BOOK DESCRIPTION

T. Duren Jones loves hiking wilderness trails. He gets out as often as he can, and enjoys taking friends and family on his explorations. Most of those who have joined his adventures still talk to him. He has hiked hundreds of trails in the American West, has summited all of the 54 Colorado 14,000 ft. peaks (now on his second round with his granddaughter), and has trekked the nearly 500 miles of the Colorado Trail's 28 segments from Denver to Durango. Once he's done with one checklist, he on to the next—this guy is nuts!

    This book is a follow-up to *Tales from the Trails*, this time with new stories presented in bite-sized pieces. Snack on a few at a time, but you might not want to put it down and end up eating, er, reading, the whole package in one sitting. As with his previous book, *Trail Mix* is part adventure, part travelogue, part motivational encouragement, part cautionary tale, and part stand-up comedy (at lest the author thinks so).

    Trail Mix is for anyone who loves spending time in the outdoors, who wishes they could be outdoors more, or who simply enjoys *reading* about nuts who spend time in the great outdoors. The author hopes by sharing these adventures—and misadventures—that the readers will be inspired to go out and discover their own stories.

TRAIL MIX

Bite sized, mostly true stories from the wilderness, featuring those who survived the author's adventures

T. DUREN JONES

WFP
WordFire Press

Trail Mix

T. Duren Jones

WordFire Press www.wordfirePress.com

ISBN: 978-1-61475-593-7

Copyright © 2018 by T. Duren Jones

Trade paperback edition August 2018

All rights reserved. No part of this book may be reproduced or transmitted in any form or by any electronic or mechanical means, including photocopying, recording or by any information storage and retrieval system, without the express written permission of the copyright holder, except where permitted by law. This novel is a work of fiction. Names, characters, places and incidents are either the product of the author's imagination, or, if real, used fictitiously.

Cover design and photos by T. Duren Jones

Kevin J. Anderson & Rebecca Moesta, Publishers

Published by WordFire Press, an imprint of WordFire, Inc. PO Box 1840 Monument, CO 80132

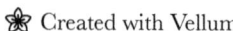 Created with Vellum

CONTENTS

1. High Adventure, Epic Fail	1
2. Rattlesnake Country, Denver	5
3. Wrestling a Mountain	9
4. Proceed at Your Own Risk	13
5. Touched by an Angel	17
6. Jurassic Park, CO	21
7. Shocking Event!	29
8. I've Got You Under My Skin	37
9. Crawling Under a Rock	39
10. The People You Meet	43
11. Lost at Lost Lakes	53
12. The Soundtrack of My Life	57
13. Slip Happens	59
14. The Monastery	63
15. Wilderness Anarchy	65
16. Creature Discomforts	71
17. Hey, Take a Hike!	75
18. Details Count	79
19. The Trail to Juvenile Delinquency	83
20. Head in the Clouds	89
21. These Were Real Buttes	93
22. Roll Out of a Predicament	97
23. Helen's Angels	99
24. For the Love of Pancakes	103
25. Meeting Moses and Zeus	107
26. Pillows and Popcorn	113
27. Lightning Fast	117
28. On Emerald Pond	125
29. The More, the Merrier!	129
30. Curses, Defoliated Again!	135
31. Succeeding at Failure	137
32. Tiny Stalker	147

33. Barking Up the Right Tree	153
34. Always Fall Season	157
35. What a Rush!	163
36. You Do Hoodoo?	179
37. Fool on a Hill	183
38. Stones of Heart	195
39. 972,000 Steps	199
Acknowledgments	203
About the Author	205

To Maren

I'd like to think I inspired my granddaughter at a young age to love the wilderness and to explore the outdoors. She now inspires me with her unbridled enthusiasm for hiking adventures. I love being part of her journey.

Chapter One

HIGH ADVENTURE, EPIC FAIL

"To succeed in life, you need two things: ignorance and confidence."—Mark Twain

BIG SANTA ANITA CANYON, SAN GABRIEL MOUNTAINS, CALIFORNIA

WE FOUND OURSELVES ON—WELL, I had carelessly led us to—a cliffy, slippery incline, with seemingly no way up or down. We were stuck. Each step on the decomposed granite felt like we were trying to climb over marbles.

I have always loved the wilderness—not just scenic drive-bys, but actually getting into the great outdoors. Growing up at the foot of the San Gabriel Mountains in Sierra Madre, California, northeast of Los Angeles, as an active latchkey lad, I was out every hot summer day, riding my Schwinn Sting-Ray bike to grand adventures. My working parents trusted my independence. And I (mostly) behaved myself—I guess that's not entirely true, but that's another story.

I explored Bailey Canyon near my house, snuck into the fenced reservoirs above the Little League field for a refreshing, prohibited swim in my underwear, built tree houses, dug holes in the backyard for dinosaur bones or buried treasure (none found, and my father—who was clearly more interested in safety than untold wealth and fame—made me fill in my unfinished archaeological sites). I pretended to be Tarzan in a Lost World of the untamed jungle section of the Los Angeles County Arboretum not far from our home, and had heroic neighborhood battles with grenade oranges and metal trash can lids, before the orange groves were converted to housing subdivisions.

Nothing changed for my love of the outdoors (except that I had fewer fruit battles) through high school and college. I could now drive to the next adventure. I hiked the Mt. Wilson Trail, trekked Eaton Canyon above Pasadena, overturned ocean tide pool rocks in a search for hidden marine surprises, camped at Joshua Tree National Park and climbed the huge boulder piles, and photojournaled the California coastline from San Diego to San Francisco. I thought of myself as quite the National Geographic explorer—a triple-combination of Sir Edmund Hillary, Jeremiah Johnson and Ansel Adams. Truly a legend in my own collegiate mind.

So it was natural that I take my friend, Diane, on a hike up to Chantry Flat in the Big Santa Anita Canyon area, not far from my home. I had an interest in being more than friends. She, unfortunately, couldn't see past my flaming red hair, having some kind of mental block against "carrot tops," perhaps after a bad childhood experience with a circus clown. But I would win her over with a demonstration of my mastery of wilderness exploration, and prowess as a trailblazer.

Chantry Flat is a designated Recreation Area in the Angeles National Forest. An 8.8 mile trail system offers scenic views, shady forested sections, abundant wildlife, a tranquil creek with large boulders, and waterfalls. It's nice that all this is available so close to the city. And it was a great place for me to show off.

At some point on the trail, and for some reason that now escapes me, I thought it was a good idea to lead us off the designated path. I know now, and probably knew then, that this is usually not a good decision. The trail is there for a reason. Not sure what I was thinking, but maybe it was for a better view of the valley below us. Or a different angle to see a waterfall below. Did I want to separate us from the other random hikers for some quiet reflection and conversation? Perhaps, I did it intentionally to put us in a dangerous situation to show how I could get us out —to save her life! In any case, here we found ourselves, on a cliff side, slippery gravel under our feet, stuck, with no clear way up or down.

Humility bears a great weight when it arrives as a result of stupid decisions. I was embarrassed. Great impression I was making! Dumb as a vegetable. More than a bit nervous, frozen really (although, stoically, I tried not to show it), with nowhere to sit, unable to move in any direction without the ground moving with us, and closer to the drop-off, we leaned against the cliff wall. Tennis shoes were not the right footwear for this hike (duh), we had no water or food as I remember, and no spend-the-night-on-the- side-of-a-cliff clothing. We evaluated our options. Diane was athletic, confident, self-reliant; I don't think she was fully looking to me to solve our dilemma. But Carrot Top, who had ignorantly gotten us into this predicament, needed to get us out.

We couldn't go back the way we came, as that was just too steep and unstable. I eyed a small shelf to our right. If we were very careful, took it slowly and deliberately, had surety with each baby step, I thought we could traverse on a diagonal back to the trail. Of course, this was coming from the guy that had gotten us into this trouble to begin with. We helped each other with hand and footholds and crept upward. Don't know if Diane could hear my heart beating through my chest.

As evidenced by this report, we made it. Clearly, Diane wasn't too put off by my bumbling attempt to impress with my wilderness recreational knowledge. She has trusted me to take her down many adventurous trails in life these past 41 years. And this is more than just a metaphor. We camped with our young kids in the valley of Yosemite, have hiked and snowshoed hundreds of trails across the American West, summited mountain peaks, trekked through the Joshua Tree and Moab deserts, and hiked over 350 miles of the Colorado Trail together.

I guess I didn't fall too flat on that first hike at Chantry Flat.

Chapter Two
RATTLESNAKE COUNTRY, DENVER

"Always carry a flagon of whiskey in case of a snakebite and furthermore always carry a small snake."—W. C. Fields

ROXBOROUGH STATE PARK, DOUGLAS COUNTY, COLORADO

I couldn't believe what I was hearing. "And watch out for rattlesnakes. Several were spotted on the trails this morning," said the too-cheerful attendant behind the visitor center counter.

Rattlesnakes? Several? I thought. *And this morning?* There was hardly anyone here today at the state park ... and there had been *several* rattlesnake sightings? I had hiked hundreds of trails in Colorado, over 26 years, and had never seen a rattlesnake. Heard they were out there. Seen none.

What exactly was I to watch out for? How? Seems like rattlesnakes were either on the trails or not. What was I suppose to do? At least when in bear country you can wear bells on your shoes to announce your coming. I guess after I paid my park fee, I should have asked about it, but in my moment of thoughtful distraction, a young mother with two antsy kids stepped up to the counter asking for three bottles of water (not flagons of whiskey). Feeling my turn in line had passed, and not wanting to scare the wee children with questions about biting snakes, I moved to the literature rack.

This was my first visit to Roxborough State Park since moving to Colorado more than two decades ago, and I wanted a trail map to get the lay of the land. Hard to believe I'm still finding new trails to explore, and with this one so close to my home near Colorado Springs—right in Denver's backyard, set up against the foothills of the Rockies. What a surprising find, with or without snakes.

Some readers believe I use a bit of hyperbole in my storytelling. But look, here's a sign in Roxborough State Park.

Roxborough is a Colorado Natural Area and a National Natural Landmark park, with close to 4,000 acres to explore. It is filled with dramatic red-rock formations, distinct ecological systems from forest to wetlands and a host of wildlife, apparently including rattlesnakes. I scanned the pamphlet rack. Surely there would be something about snakes.

Published by the Colorado Division of Wildlife, a wide range of helpful literature on display included "Don't Feed the Wildlife" (wasn't in my plans—I know better from personal experience), "Living with Bears" (no intention to—no interest, and they make terrible house guests) and "Your Guide to Avoiding Human-Coyote Conflicts" (just don't start arguments with them about religion, politics, and social issues). But no brochures on rattlesnake encounters, which seemed like quite an omission, given the disconcerting warning from the park representative.

I did learn that visitors can take in all of Roxborough's geological wonders via a network of interconnected trails for every level of your hiking ability. I started out on the Willow Creek Trail, which would connect me to the South Rim Trail loop. I was glad to see that no trail was named "Rattlesnake Gulch," "Venom Valley," or "Snakebite Creek." A hundred yards or so in, I stumbled (not literally) upon some kind of red-faced youth corps worker lying spread-eagle on the ground, possibly the victim of a deadly serpent attack.

"Just resting," she responded to my concerned inquiry by smiling, waving and saying she was okay. I had to take her word for it.

I rounded shady turns and discovered more young people along the side of the trail. I learned that they were volunteering their time for trail maintenance, and that they were simply taking it easy before their successive turn on a fireman bucket brigade of wheelbarrow loads of dirt. I thanked them for their trail work, although I wondered how much they were actually getting done in the heat of the mid-day.

Roxborough State Park reminded me of the red-rock beauty of Garden of the Gods in the Springs, but not commercialized, not crowded, and carpeted with wildflowers and lush emerald green everywhere. The trails are easy to moderate in difficulty and are laid out with scenic viewpoints in mind. They go from wet lands to prairie to mountain foothills, and weave around monolithic red sandstone formations that tilt at a 60-degree angle. After I left the exhausted, sun-stroked workers, I had the place nearly all to myself.

This day I saw deer, birds, a rabbit, butterflies, a red fox and a fuzzy-wuzzy caterpillar, but no rattlesnakes. Perhaps that would have made a better story, one of valiant survival in the wilderness (like some of those in my *Tales from the Trails* book), with me on all fours, dragging my bitten, bloody, swollen leg for miles on newly repaired trails, only to find the visitor center closed for the day.

Chapter Three
WRESTLING A MOUNTAIN

"Laughter can bring a new perspective."—Christopher Durang

MOUNT YALE (14,199 FT.), COLLEGIATE PEAKS, SAWATCH RANGE, COLORADO

I WAS JUST another father concerned about who was dating his only daughter. I may have been a little overprotective, I'll admit. I own a shotgun for bird hunting and skeet shooting, and I let each young man know that. And that it's loaded.

When I first met Joe, I wasn't sure who this guy was, his background, or who he'd turn out to be one day. I did know that Sarah and Joe hadn't met at church or school youth group, but at a raucous dance club. And that he was older than Sarah, by a few years—more than a few. Maybe not this dad's first choice for a future son-in-law, but I was willing to give him the benefit of my doubts. I took my finger off the trigger.

I'm not going to say that Joe was immediately a kiss-up to my wife Diane, and me—I'll let you draw your own conclusions. Okay, forget that: This guy was a real kiss-up, lips fully puckered.

I was working in the front yard, moving a delivered pile of dirt around for a driveway island. Joe had just arrived with Sarah and proceeded to introduce himself. I put the shovel and shotgun down and shook his powerful hand. He shared that he was preparing for competition at the Olympic Training Center in Colorado Springs as a wrestler. I shook the pain out of my hand and picked the gun back up.

We chatted for a few minutes. Joe asked what I was doing, and I explained, even though I thought it seemed pretty obvious.

"I love yard work! Especially moving dirt around!" he said, as he grabbed up another, larger shovel and started helping. I barely stifled laughter.

I told him I had also picked up rocks at the local landscaping yard to build a small retaining wall. I had used the cargo section of my vintage, 1976 International Scout SUV.

"I love old International Scouts!" he exclaimed. "And, as I'm also a mechanic, I can help you with any repairs! I love working on Scouts! Need anything fixed?"

My wife came out with a pitcher of ice-cold lemonade for a refresh on this hot day. Joe had already flung dirt hard enough to work up a sweat. "Thank you sooo much! I love lemonade!" Why did that not surprise me?

Hmmmm ... do I shoot him now, or wait? This was quite entertaining. And it was kinda hard *not* to like this guy. *Maybe I'll hold off a while.*

A few weeks later, we were talking with Sarah and Joe about our son, Cary, and plans to climb our next Colorado 14,000-ft. peak. "I love hiking and mountain climbing!" Joe said. He shared some experiences from his low-elevation Georgia home.

"Do ... you ... want ... to join us ... next weekend?" I asked, knowing the answer.

"I'd LOVE to!"

Joe had never climbed a 14er before and had not even hiked in these Rocky Mountains, as far as I knew. But he was strong, athletic, in good condition. I didn't worry about his ability to do this. We started our drive to the trailhead before dawn toward Buena Vista and the Collegiate Peak group of mountains where Mt. Yale was located.

I didn't have as many extra supplies then as I do now. I provided Joe with what I had, a canvas Swiss fanny pack that flapped and spanked him up the trail. It became so annoying to him—amusing to us—that I tied it onto my larger pack for the rest of the nine-mile round trip.

The well-worn trail finally broke out of the forest, providing a wonderful high alpine encounter, with spectacular views. The climb was relatively moderate in difficulty, until the bit of boulder hopping and scrambling around rocky points near the summit.

Joe did great. He took no more rest breaks up than we did. He may have talked the whole time, much more than we usually do. Perhaps Joe was a bit nervous. But it was enjoyable, with his Southern drawl and quick wit. And, of course, he *loved* this experience.

It wasn't until we were back at the car that he told us he had worked out too hard at the Olympic Center the previous day and had pulled a hamstring. We knew nothing about this! He had been in terrible pain the whole hike but had never complained and would not have quit, ever. He had wrestled that mountain all the way to the top. That showed real character … or real foolishness. Maybe I *would* shoot him when we got home. You know, like putting a wounded animal out of its misery.

Some time has passed. Cary, Joe and I still tell the Mt. Yale story, and Joe's painful introduction to our outdoor-loving family. Joe is an important part of our life now—good husband to our daughter, great daddy to our granddaughter, hard worker, a friend as much as a son-in-law, a hiking buddy, and a constant source of entertainment. He makes us laugh, a lot. We LOVE this guy!

YEARS LATER, WE CAME BACK AND CLIMBED THE SAME PEAK VIA a different route, but this time with my very enthusiastic, overly-caffeinated, extremely-chatty granddaughter Maren (recounted in another chapter in this book). Joe and I have aged a bit and put on a few pounds, but for the most part, we were able to keep up with our athletic-teen … if she waited for us.

Chapter Four

PROCEED AT YOUR OWN RISK

"You may also be exposed to unreasonable acts of others."
—Warning sign entering the National Forest

ST. MARY'S GLACIER, ARAPAHO NATIONAL FOREST, COLORADO

The "Avalanche Hazard" caution blazed yellow on wood posts at the base of the mountain. It was hard to ignore the sign posted by the U.S. Forest Service, right in the middle of our snowshoe trail. Seemed it was worth a stop to read.

I had never climbed St. Mary's Glacier in the Rocky Mountains, just a few miles west of Denver. The glacier is a semi-permanent snowfield in the Arapaho National Forest at about 11,000 feet. We had a heavy snowfall all winter in the high country, everything around us was a snowfield.

My nephew, Wyatt, and I had ben ichin' for a snowshoe hike do-over. A couple of weeks before, in another part of the state, we failed miserably getting into the high country, taking a blizzard spanking. Climbing a glacier this April morning seemed like an interesting challenge. And the weather was nice.

The bright sign warned of potentially dangerous avalanches or snow slide paths, and said to proceed at your own risk. But the notice didn't stop there. The fine print disclaimer read (I kid you not):

"Access Point Notice to Backcountry Travellers—Hazards are not limited to, but include: changing weather conditions, landslides, caves, overlooks, falling tree limbs, high or rushing water, contaminated water, wild animals, becoming lost, overexertion, hypothermia, remnants of mines, tunnels and shafts, decaying structures, and changing trail conditions …."

And …

"You may also be exposed to unreasonable acts of others."

Wait … what? Who wouldn't just turn around at this point and hike back to their car? Walking into a Denver biker bar with a loony grin, wearing a birthday hat, holding up a rubber chicken, and shouting that Harley riders are sissies, sounds safer to me.

And what exactly are "unreasonable acts of others," in the context of wilderness trekking? By definition, unreasonable means uncooperative, not guided by good sense, not fair, irrational, out of touch with practical reality, and inappropriate attitude or behavior. And I may be exposed to such individuals on the trails? I don't have to go into the wilds to encounter this… I could have just stayed home and scrolled through political posts on Facebook!

So what do these unreasonable acts look like up in the mountains? Would a hiker I met be hoarding a trail, and not sharing? Would someone be encouraging others to take unnecessary risks ("Sure, you can make it. Take a running jump from cliff edge to cliff edge over that raging creek!")? And could I encounter naked hikers (that seems inappropriate), those changing directional signs on purpose, any hikers chasing unicorns and fairies through fields of wildflowers, or someone standing on a boulder shouting claim to the mountain in the name of Ming the Merciless? No further instructions were given for what I'm suppose to do when I am exposed to such individuals.

Despite the unwelcoming advice to hikers, Wyatt and I looked at each other and with a smile, we cautiously pressed on. Snow clouds built ominously around us, fresh snow powdered the surrounding peaks. But the sun broke through in patches where we ascended the steep glacier slope. Curiously—and perhaps telling—no other snowshoe prints preceded us. It seemed like no one had been on the glacier in some time, perhaps wisely heeding the advice on the notice below.

Near the several-hundred-foot elevation gain to the top, we watched snow blow off the cornice overhangs on adjoining ridges. To hike up further would mean crossing the remaining section, rather than staying close to the boulders at the edge. A layer of new spring snow on the winter pack seemed likely to break loose.

I try to use good judgment in the high country. I've turned back on numerous occasions from a peak summit due to bad weather. But I'm also goal-driven, tenacious, with an insatiable curiosity as to what's around the next bend or what I might see from the top. And, probably a little stupid at times too.

I decided to test the snow. I really did want to see the sights from the top of the glacier. I had Wyatt stay back by the security of the boulders and started out on a diagonal across the snow field. So far, so good, for about 50 yards. The snow seemed stable … and then it didn't. I felt a little movement. Maybe the snow slipping was just my imagination. Perhaps a tremble from within, as I began to have serious thoughts about this being a good idea for me or my 17-year old nephew. There it was again: the very slightest of movement, and a short, dull growl well beneath my snowshoes. Those unreasonable hikers that are willing to proceed at this point are the ones also asking to be removed from the gene pool. I turned around and quickly headed back to the edge of the glacier.

Although I had wanted to go higher and farther, to see the panoramic views from the top, we decided not to "proceed at our own risk" at this point. Our families, and search and rescue teams, would thank us.

Wyatt and I headed back to the trailhead and just hoped that we wouldn't be exposed to the unreasonable acts of others on our way out. That might be worse than an avalanche.

Chapter Five

TOUCHED BY AN ANGEL

"Insight is better than eyesight when it comes to seeing an angel."—Eileen Elias Freeman

MT. SHAVANO, SAWATCH RANGE, COLORADO

HAVE YOU EVER ENCOUNTERED AN ANGEL? I have. Lest you think I'm some wacky mystic, let me explain.

To see this angel you *do* have to go up, up, up to thinner air, to higher country. You can't have a personal experience with her from the valley or the roadside. You have to work for it—literally climb a mountain for this discovery.

The angel I refer to is the Angel of Shavano, a shallow, snow-filled gully, with two diverging branches at the top—two upstretched arms in the center of Mt. Shavano's (14,231 ft.) east slopes. The Angel is a herald that directs the way to the top.

At my age, I take frequent, quick rest stops when ascending a 14er—you have to, as every cell in your body is screaming for air with each steep step upwards. At certain intervals, I'll take a little longer break for fuel (energy snacks) and hydration. On this climb, I was all alone and in no hurry to summit as the weather was perfect, warm with a Colorado blue bird sky. So, on one stop, I decided to rest in the shade of a scraggly, wind-twisted pine at tree line. I may have even fallen asleep for a few minutes as a gentle breeze rustled the high alpine grass next to me. Wispy cirrus clouds began to glide by and a couple of crows rode the morning thermals in large sweeping circles higher and higher. I was so enjoying this little glimpse of Heaven, but it was time for me to get moving again.

The body of the Angel rises from 12,000 feet to 12,800 feet. As you ascend her snow slope (she doesn't mind, really, although it may feel a little improper), at the top of the body, you must choose an arm. The southern arm leads to a 13,380-foot saddle; the northern arm leads directly toward the summit. Both point the way to the top of the mountain and the clouds beyond.

This mountain is part of the Sawatch Range that runs through the heart of the Colorado Rockies. Both the northernmost and southernmost Sawatch fourteeners, Mount of the Holy Cross and Mount Shavano, have snow features with religious significance. For both peaks, it requires an effort to locate these symbols on the mountainside. They're not Indiana Jones-like discoveries, but seeing these natural treasures on the sides of mountains is still an extraordinary experience.

Whether hiking through woods, trekking across rolling hills and flower-carpeted meadows, or climbing mountainsides, every turn in the path on these journeys can offer new and different views, varied with fresh perspectives, beautiful and wondrous things to see and do. But the wilderness doesn't give up these experiences without an investment. We make the effort, and the reward isn't just in reaching the destination, but also in the joy of discovery along the way.

Cherished outdoor experiences await us. But I won't find them sitting on my couch, nor from the National Geographic Channel, and not by cruising past a scenic location at 65 miles an hour on the highway. True discovery in the wilderness requires getting *out there* to explore—putting some distance between ourselves and noise and sight pollution of the city, taking the time to walk a path to a panoramic vista, turning a rock over to look under it, sitting so still in the forest that a woodland critter doesn't even know we are there.

On a mountainside, or back in the valley with the civilized, if

I'm not making new discoveries every day, maybe I'm not making the effort. Life is ready to reveal itself. It's a sacred promise. A contract. Perhaps I need to get my rear end off the La-Z-Boy more and prepare to go deeper, higher, farther. Who knows what grand views, surprises and adventures are waiting around each next bend?

Angels, we're told, are messengers. Perhaps the message to me from the Angel of Shavano was that great experiences await me in the future. But not without sacrifice.

Chapter Six
JURASSIC PARK, CO

"Every time I'm sad, I try to imagine a T-Rex trying to put on a hat."—Unknown

PICKET WIRE CANYONLANDS, PURGATOIRE RIVER VALLEY, COLORADO

THERE IS NOT much to see in the remote southeast plains of Colorado—that is, unless you want to dig deeper. I did, and was rewarded for the effort.

I've trekked into the Colorado wilderness quite a bit—mostly in the mountains—but I'm still making new discoveries. One recent spring, I headed out to the Comanche National Grasslands (lots of grass, but no Comanches that I could see) to hike in the Picket Wire Canyonlands and the Purgatoire River Valley—the waterway apparently named by French trappers who spelled words funny. Until recently, I didn't know that this area was home to the largest set of dinosaur tracks in North America. This, I had to see.

I drove (what seemed like) millions of miles from home, and millions of years back in time, eons and eons before the first stake was ever driven into soil in what would become Colorado Springs. This was barren country except for the occasional piñon pine, antelope herd and jackrabbit rushing across the dirt road ahead of my tires that were throwing up dust behind me. The directions to the trailhead took me miles this way, then that way, then another direction altogether, the four-wheel-drive roads getting progressively worse the farther I went. I was a long way from my mountains; for all practical purposes, I might as well have been in northeastern New Mexico, and transported back in time.

I halted to take my first photo of the day, amused at what I saw. At a T in the road, there stood a leaning, rusty stop sign. I looked one way, then the other, surmising that I could see about 100 miles in both directions across the gentle, rolling hills. No other vehicles glistened in the soft morning light. A stop sign ... okay. That was surprising.

Nothing was out there, not even a bush large enough for an outdoor potty break, following that second cup of morning coffee. I could see perhaps why the dinosaurs wanted to leave here, hoping to head west to the beaches of Southern California. And they might have made it except for those pesky Rockies. Tough getting that bulk up and over the mountain passes, I guess. (I know, the mountains may not have even been there yet, but I liked the illustration.)

I imagined the difficulty of the early pioneers moving west, and the Mexican settlers to this area. There is such *aloneness* out here, which I like, compared to my civilized work-a-day world. But a sense of *vulnerability* as well. I half expected, when I started out on the trail, that I would immediately see vultures circling overhead, forks and knives in steely claws, cotton napkins tied around their necks.

I finally made it to the Picket Wire Corrals, and at this point the route finding became difficult. Most visitors to this remote area enter the canyon from another direction, and with a scheduled U.S. Forest Service guide, caravanning their vehicles in. As I continued, the driving trail marker signs didn't match the numbered road directions I had printed out from Internet sites. Nothing on my rudimentary map made sense, so I stopped after a split in the rutted road to review my notes.

A little white sedan with two women unexpectedly passed me, and waved. *Hmmm...they seem to know where they are going*, I thought. *I'll follow them.* This was a good place to park, so I hydrated, got my day pack together, pulled out my hiking stick, sprayed myself with sunscreen, put on my broad-brimmed hat, and I was off. It was a longer trek than expected to catch up to my new guides in the white sedan.

A genesis of yellow spring wildflower blooms greeted me along the serpentine road. I could see storm clouds building from the northwest. I knew I could expect rain but hoped it would hold off until the forecasted afternoon hours. When I did come upon the white car, the occupants were out and busy doing *something.*

"Hello!" I called, not wanting to startle them.

"Stop! Stop right there! Don't move!" the older, taller of two women yelled at me. I complied. This was still the Wild, Wild West in some respects.

She then turned to the scrub brush around her and shouted something garbled, but to me it sounded a bit like Brutus or Bruiser or Buttkiss. She screamed again. No response. I stood frozen.

Out bounded two monster dogs, breed mixes I didn't recognize, but by their mouthful of saber teeth, they looked to be a combination of Rottweiler and Velociraptor. Tall Woman barely grabbed the collar of one of the snarling dogs; her younger, heavier friend or daughter snagged the other. I thought the effort would prove useless as the women were dragged a few feet when the dogs fought to charge at me.

"It's ... it's okay now," Tall Woman sputtered, barely heard over the barking. "We got 'em."

The struggle with her beast did not instill confidence. Who brings an aggressive dog, or dogs, out into the wilderness, especially without a leash? Especially with teeth like that? (The dog, not the woman.) But I said nothing.

"They are okay," the younger spoke. "Friendly, really, after they get to know you." *Or after they eat you.* "We bring them with us for security."

No kidding. I had little doubt that the dogs were effective. But it was ridiculous not to keep them under tight control. I approached cautiously and saw that the women had brought a pantry-full of food for brunch, placing it all on the hood of their car.

I explained that I was uncertain about the directions to the trailhead and asked if they knew more. With great sureness, Tall Woman pointed and stated that the trail down to the canyon and river below was just a bit farther, to the left. I was to follow the last of the rough, dirt road and would clearly see my way down. I believed it was inevitable that when I rounded the corner, out of sight, the two would release the Hounds of Hell to make a meal out of me.

Walking for a quarter mile, I could see no good trail down through the cliffs from this plateau, about a 300-foot drop to the valley floor. So making a loop, I ended up right back at the white car, and the killer dogs. I expressed with some frustration that I had seen no trail. Younger One said, "Just over there. On yer left. We were here last year and found it."

I made another loop. With my hiking experience, I could have navigated a route down the cliffs, but surely that way could not be any public hiking trail. Back to the car, I showed the ladies my map and trail description. Over the barking, I told them this was not where they thought they were, and that I was returning to my car to drive back to the start.

"Hmmm," Tall Woman said, as she stuffed the last of a sandwich in her mouth and chased it with a big swig of two-liter Diet Coke. "Could have sworn this was the place. Maybe you are right."

Do you think?

This detour had added at least an extra mile to my hiking day and cost me almost an hour of lost time. Lesson learned: Don't put your trust in sedan-driving, big-dogs-off-leash pet owners who are confused and disoriented, clearly having no idea where they are, yet willing to give advice to others. Close to the Purgatoire River Valley, how do you say "idiots" in French?

I drove back the way I came, trying to avoid large mud puddles from heavy rain the day before. I don't know how I missed them coming in, but on my left were campers cooking breakfast over a smoky fire. Both had camouflage clothing on (maybe that's how I missed them!)—surely *they* would know the surroundings. I got out of car and shouted a greeting. The father and son had been turkey hunting. I explained my dilemma of trying to find the trail down to the valley.

"Do you want the harder trail or the easier one?" the dad asked. "The harder way is back there. Just stay to the left at the Y in the road, and it will take you right to the trailhead."

Of course! The Y in the road. The dog ladies had taken the right side branch at the junction!

"And the easier route?" I inquired.

"You leave from right here. Through that opening in the brush. Not marked anywhere." He pointed. "Trail's on your left in a couple hundred yards. Look for the white rocks to start down. This trail will take you right to the old cemetery, and the dirt road to the dinosaur tracks."

The old cemetery?

The ruins of a Spanish mission were one of the sites I wanted to see! I would miss the Indian petroglyphs by taking this route, but I had seen that type of Native American rock art in southwest Utah. Frankly, although I admire the prehistoric, nomadic hunter-gatherers' ability to survive in such desolate regions, I'm not too impressed with their artistic ability. Being a graphic designer and artist myself, I feel I'm qualified to critique. Where were the da Vincis of their time? To their credit, they were using rock chisels and rock hammers to draw on, well, rock. I guess they did their best.

Glad to be back on track, I quickly readied myself, started out again, looked back to wave goodbye at my more-dependable trail advisors, and promptly stepped into a cactus, driving a large needle through the side mesh of my boot and straight into my foot. I dared show no pain, disguising my limp as a spring in my step because of my enthusiasm for finding the trail. Around a corner, and out of sight, I gasped, took off my boot and removed the spike with tweezers from my trusty Swiss Army knife.

A rocky path switchbacked down the cliffs, rimmed by sparse piñon and juniper forests, into a canyon deeply cut out of the landscape. I didn't think many hikers came this way. Because this wasn't a designated trail, I thought I should leave breadcrumbs to find my way back. I decided instead to set up some small rock cairns along the way; birds wouldn't be tempted to eat these. The trail "flattened out" to rolling hills channeled by the cliffs on either sides, and eventually opened up to a broad valley, starting to spring green.

Sure enough, my rugged trail spilled out right at the cemetery and the dirt road that would lead to the dino tracks. The Dolores Mission and Cemetery was built and maintained between 1871 and 1889. Some remains are still visible. A small sign instructs visitors not to tip over the few remnant grave markers. Glad that warning was there, otherwise, I might have been tempted to knock them all over. Seriously, anyone who makes the effort to travel this far into the wilderness, to visit historic sites, needs such an admonition?

The Purgatoire River etched out this colorful valley, exposing rock layers of prehistoric sea beds and an ancient lakeshore where the dinosaurs roamed long before the buffalo. About that river's name, according to legend, a group of Spanish treasure-seeking soldiers died in the canyons without the benefit of clergy. So, in the sixteenth century the river was named El Rio de Las Animas Perdidas en Purgatorio (The River of Lost Souls in Purgatory). Later, French trappers shortened the name of the waterway to Purgatoire. And later, less Continental Anglo travelers on the Santa Fe Trail that could not pronounce "Purgatoire" (and didn't care for the attitude of the French) began to call the canyonlands Picket Wire, for reasons known only to them.

It was nearly two miles on the dirt road to the dinosaur tracks. Small birds—thankfully, not famished vultures—darted from bush to bush. The storm clouds built into dark, threatening shapes—beautiful, really, despite the possible dread they foretold —but I wouldn't need to worry about them until my drive home.

The destination did not disappoint. The quarter-mile stretch of footprints along the banks of the river was amazing. Over 1,300 dinosaur prints in 100 separate trackways tell the story of these beasts moving westward along the muddy edge of a vast freshwater lake. Their footprints were eventually buried and turned to stone. Roughly 60 percent of the tracks were left by the allosaurus, a two-footed, three-toed, meat-eating scavenger that possibly hunted in packs. The balance were left by the mighty brontosaurus, a four-footed plant eater.

It looked like in the 1,300 dino prints left for us to view, that there may have been a lot of pushing and shoving on their movement along the lake.

Scientists say the site tells us something about the social behavior of dinosaurs. For example, parallel tracks seem to show that several young brontosaurus were traveling together as a group along the shoreline. There was evidence that the rowdy group of dino teens was loud, smoked, and had committed some acts of vandalism. I just made that up. No scientific studies support that. What all the footprints *did* show was that it looked like there was a lot of pushing and shoving on their way west, and that some of the clade Dinosauria had digested some fermented berries, making their path look like it was made by a 39-ton drunken pioneer.

I would have stayed longer exploring the river's edge, but several four-wheel-drive vehicles arrived at the rustic, wilderness parking area and spilled out loudly enthusiastic schoolchildren with lunch bags, all led by a Forest Service guide. If you don't hike in, the only other way to experience the valley is with a pre-arranged guide. Good for the children—I wish I had discovered something like this as a kid. But, like our dino friends from eons past, it was time for me to go. I'm a solitary, two-footed, meat-eating adventurer who enjoys his peace and quiet.

 I reflected on my time at the Purgatoire River site on my wet drive home—the clouds opened up a deluge. I thought about the uninformed misdirection that started my expedition that day and wondered if the *idiots* had ever found their way back to the actual trailhead. I chuckled—but then I remembered plenty of times when that word had described me too. People who live in glass houses shouldn't throw dinosaur bones.

Chapter Seven
SHOCKING EVENT!

"I'm not anxious. I am just extremely well educated about all the things that can go catastrophically wrong."—Anonymous

CHEYENNE MOUNTAIN, ABOVE COLORADO SPRINGS, PIKE NATIONAL FOREST

THE AFTERNOON HAD ALL the signs and potential of things going very wrong. I have had plenty of first-hand experience with nasty weather in Colorado. I know what *can* happen, how many ways things can go bad. It's not knowing how exactly to plan for the *unexpected* that makes me anxious at times.

We all knew something was moving in on the mountain—local radar warned of the coming summer thunderstorm system to the region. I had been alerted by Dispatch over the walkie-talkies to keep my eyes pealed for lightning. As a Wilderness Driver for the Broadmoor Hotel's mountain guest resort, Cloud Camp, above Colorado Springs, I was on my fourth trip up and down the 16 switchbacks on the dirt road that day with guests. What happened on Cheyenne Mountain that day *was* unexpected! And, a first for me!

To roll out the story, maybe I'll start by putting it to song. I'll provide the lyrics, you'll have to come up with the music in your head.

The Wreck of the Escalade Cadillac
(with thanks to Gordon Lightfoot, "The Wreck of the Edmund Fitzgerald")

The legend lives on from Denver on down
Of the big mountain they call Cheyenne
The Mount, it is said, never gives up its dead
When the skies of August turn gloomy
With a load of two guests and one staff more
Than the Caddie weighed empty
That great SUV and driver were a open target
When the afternoon thunderstorm came in early
The car was the pride of Broadmoor Hotel rides
Coming down from Camping in the Clouds
As SUVs go, it was bigger than most
With an experienced motorist well seasoned
Assigned to transport visitors, bodies needing relax
When they rode half-loaded (seats seven) for the
    Hotel Spa
Nearly at the bottom, all got their bells rung
Could that be lightning they were seein'?

Wind drove rain making a tatter-tatter sound
Bright light flashed off by cliff's edge
And everyone knew, as the driver did too
T'was Zeus that had come bolt throwin'
The storm came fast and the massage would have to wait
Colorado summer monsoons hit fiercely
And when arrived, often electrified
In the face of the maelstrom all sat shocked

When the screaming stopped, the red-haired driver asked
Everyone, is everybody okay?
At two thirty seven, after the hit, the passenger window
    dropped down
Guests, glad you are all safe, he said

TRAIL MIX

The driver called the hotel while rain water poured in
The good car and passengers still in peril
Frozen ride rolled to a stop, engine fried, and thus
Came the wreck of the Escalade Cadillac

In a sparkling office in Detroit they planned
With great interest engineers had to know
Phones rang, information was shared many times
Each GM exec curious about a direct lightning strike
The legend now lives on from Denver on down
Of the big mountain they call Cheyenne
The Mount, it is said, never gives up its dead
Well, a luxury SUV can be resurrected for 35 grand

I WAS TAKING A FAMILY OF FIVE UP THE FORMERLY-NAMED Cheyenne Highway to Cloud Camp, a recently constructed luxury mountain resort, built on the Cheyenne Mountain Lodge ruins. This private dirt trail-road climbs approximately 3,000 feet in a little over 2 miles from the base of the mountain. Built in the 1920s by the Broadmoor's founder, Spencer Penrose (who also built the original lodge), this challenging road to the top is made up of 16 tight turns, and was listed in the Guinness Book of World Records as the steepest set of switchbacks in North America.

The driving staff take guests up and down the mountain in Cadillac Escalades because, well, frankly, they are 5-Star, 5-Diamond Broadmoor Hotel guests. The vehicles are also very sure-footed for this off-road use, especially with varied seasonal snow, ice, hail or mud, with their full four-wheel-drive features, built on a Suburban chassis. Still, they are expensive, and probably not built for this type of daily use.

The family I was transporting in style was excited to come to the mule stables on our way up for their stay. One of the boys was here for his birthday celebration. The parents had made plans for a surprise mule ride up the trail to the lodge for the young lad. When I slowed to a stop, I got a radio transmission in my ear bud that because lightning had been sighted, I needed to cancel the ride and get the guests up to the safety of the lodge.

They were disappointed, but understood, and could reschedule the mule experience. Better safe than singed.

My passengers for the ride down from the lodge included a staff member—her first time on the mountain—and two guests going to the hotel for a pampering spa appointment. Dark clouds formed all around us. By the time we were halfway down, we were in the thick of it, surrounded by bright flashes of light and huge, simultaneous thunderclaps. It's rough, weather-wise, at these higher elevations in Colorado. Two weeks earlier, one of the camp's mules was struck by lightning, killing it instantly.

Halfway between Switchbacks No. 3 and No. 4, my Caddie took a direct lightning strike. We all had seen in periphery vision the bright explosion off to our cliffside right— like a transformer exploding in a tornado—and immediately heard and felt the ka-boom that made you want to duck for cover.

The mind works so fast, but I was having trouble processing just what was happening. Huge sparks like fireworks bounced progressively from the rear of the SUV to the front, bam, bam, bam, blowing off the passenger-side rearview mirror. Funny, for a micro moment, I thought someone was shooting at us, having never experience anything like this before.

I didn't have a choice of stopping the vehicle on the narrow road—it did that for me. The engine, steering wheel, gear shifter, brakes, the wheels, everything on the dash board, all froze up in an instant. All of the electronics were fried, and smoke was rising from burnt wires in the engine compartment. For some reason, the right front passenger window dropped down, and the driving rain whooshed in. We all thought at first that the window had blown out like the mirror had blown off, but there was no broken glass shards anywhere.

From the front passenger seat, our new staffer undid her seatbelt and leapt between the two guests and into the back-back seat. I first checked to see if everyone was okay, before considering the auto damage. That was good of me. I was reassuring the guests, and the guests were comforting the staff person. Everyone was fine, but all now sat stunned at what had just happened. It was shocking, really (sorry for that). We realized we had just taken a direct hit, a lightning bolt at a temperature of roughly 53,000 degrees—hotter than the surface of the sun—had just zapped us! I called in to my supervisors (I had a walkie-talkie and could get cell phone connection) to announce what had happened. They had never got a call like that.

It was humorous that the Escalade seemed to want to try to hold on like some kind of broken, dying robot. The interior and dashboard lights, as well as the headlights, would just randomly turn on and off. The window washer fluid would come by itself on and spray for a while. Finally, the car just sighed, shook, coughed, and died.

The passengers were, understandably, shaken. Of course, I'm thinking that this is going to make a great story! How many can say their car was struck by lightning? And lived to tell about it? The vehicle's framework acted, as it was designed, as a Faraday Cage and sent all the electricity around us and down into the ground. Thank you automotive engineers.

As an interesting side note, there is a landscape photographer in the Springs, Larry Marr, who also does a fabulous job of capturing images of dramatic weather conditions in the Pikes Peak Region. That day, he could see the storm closing in on Cheyenne Mountain, got out his telephoto lens camera, and started shooting. He later posted photos on his Facebook site of the lightning on the mountain—one, a composite image of multiple strikes on the top. But, unbelievably, one single-image shot he posted showed the actual strike that got my Escalade! It was time dated 2:37 pm, and showed the exact spot where we were hit. I not only had the experience, but now have a photo of the event as well!

When the rain subsided, I got out of the Caddie to assess the damage. I was surprised that I didn't see any burnt spots along the side of the vehicle. I was sure I'd see something like bored holes and a still smoking streak along the side where the lightning traveled. The only evidence was the sight of fragments of the mirror hanging by a few wires.

I walked on the road about twenty yards back where I thought we were hit, seeing if I could piece the event together. Evidence told the story. It looked like the lightning first hit a large pine, ripping and burning it down the center. The bolt exploded into the ground, throwing up dirt and gravel out of its own self-made pit. Then, in uncanny coincidental timing, just as we passed, the electrical charge jumped up to the metal of our passing vehicle. The percentage chance of something like that happening seems astronomical!

It took quite a while for the tow truck to reach us. Apparently, with all the strikes on the mountain, power was lost at the main gate to the trail road, and no one knew how to open the gate manually. The guests missed their spa appointment. They decided they just wanted to return to the bar at the lodge for an adult beverage to relax. I couldn't blame them, and another vehicle was sent down from camp to take them back up. Curiously, felt a strong connection to my new survival partners. We had a near-death experience together. Maybe we'd be bonded through our shared endurance story. Become Facebook Friends. Celebrate the holidays. Vacation together. They never call.

Word of my electrifying event had made it all around to the hotel staff before I even got back. Somehow, and in a flash, the moniker "Lightning Boy" was attached to me, and so was I greeted in the hallways upon my return. Real funny.

One of my department managers said, "Tim, trouble seems to follow you!" Now, in context, this *had* been the year that I slipped on ice at one of the camps and broke my wrist (read that knee-slapping chapter in this book), had a huge tree branch fall on the roof of another Escalade in a wind storm, and I narrowly avoided a monster boulder that had rolled down the mountain onto the road.

I don't go looking for trouble, and I'm pretty sure it's not deliberately seeking me out. Still, the evidence seems to speak for itself. But, I don't want to be "That Guy." The one coming down the hallway, and someone says, "Hey, look, it's Tim. And look what's following him: It's Trouble!" Who needs that?

I would have thought that the Cadillac Escalade guest transport would have been "toast," completely totaled. It was taken to the local dealership for inspection and repair. GM even sent out engineers to see how their vehicles did with a direct lightning strike. I guess that's not something you can test at the factory, being hotter than the sun and all. Weeks later, and with $35,000 in fixes (that's about what my first home cost!), the luxury SUV was back in the fleet, as good as new.

People ask me, if at the time, I felt anything. Or even now, if I have any residual issues.

The answer is no. Nothing, really. Nada. Well, that is if you ignore the (more than usual) pale skin, my consistently unruly hair standing on end, and that occasional annoying twitch sending my head into one shoulder. I like to think of it all adding to my electric personality.

And not a hair out of place (maybe raised a little higher). Note the blown-apart side mirror.

Chapter Eight
I'VE GOT YOU UNDER MY SKIN

"I don't care how small or big they are, insects freak me out."—Alexander Wang

BIG CEDAR WILDERNESS TRAILS, DALLAS, TEXAS

A COUPLE OF YEARS AGO, I was in Texas for some contract work and a family visit. I was able to take my granddaughter Maren with me. Of course, we had to find a trail to hike.

I found out that everything in this state wants to bite, sting, pinch or burrow into you. No wonder residents (except the most hardcore hikers, marathon runners or fat-tire bikers) spend most of their time in the air-conditioned, hermetically sealed shopping malls.

Even before we ventured out into the wilderness, I had so many mosquito bites I looked to be in the advanced stages of chicken pox. The evil little suckers must have sensed new, out-of-town blood. They attacked with stealth and showed no mercy. I'm surprised I didn't need a blood transfusion by week's end. Look, I know there is a place for insects in nature's ecosystem. And with such creepy-crawlies, I usually say, "live and let live." I just don't want them living on or in me! Maren seemed to have escaped for the most part.

Prior to the hike we found in Big Cedar Wilderness Trails (BCWT), my Texs family warned us of other crawling and flying nuisances. We were advised to use bug spray liberally. We might encounter biting flies, ticks, fire ants, wasps, chiggers (which, I learned with great consternation, go for the moist, dark places and dig in under the skin), rattlesnakes and the dreaded "No-See-Ums." *Wait, what? There are such things?* Yes, it says it right on the bug spray can label. *And you can't even see them?*

No-See-Ums, or Ceratopogonidae, are a gnat-like fly, smaller than fleas, barely visible to the naked eye, and are also known as biting midges, sand flies, punkies or, as I called them, "vicious little buggers from the depths of hell." Google the bite photos, if you dare. The bugs are so small they can get through screens on windows and doors. Their bite is painful, causing welts that last for days, and they can get up into a person's mouth, nose, eyes and ears. I sprayed bug spray all over myself like a fire hose … and then did it again, including places I don't want to talk about.

Big Cedar Wilderness Trails, just outside Dallas, is located atop one of the most breathtaking bluffs in North Texas. The multi-use, 21-mile trail system winds through cedar and hardwood forests and descends into a valley with a striking elevation change. The valley consists mostly of mesquite trees and cacti. BCWT has ten trail loops ranging from beginner to advanced. They all detour off and return to the main trail with easy access to the parking lot.

We really enjoyed these hiking trails, so far away and so different from those in our home state of Colorado. And any concerns about biting, stinging, blistering insects turned out to be not much of an issue. That may, no doubt, have been due to our thorough saturation of DEET bug repellant. Our biggest concern was about mountain bikers buzzing past us at 90 miles per hour, and "hitchhiking" burs and stickers covering our boots, socks, shorts and shirts. These bugged us more than the insects.

Chapter Nine
CRAWLING UNDER A ROCK

"You will do foolish things, but do them with enthusiasm."—Colette

MT. COLUMBIA, 14,078 FT., COLLEGIATE PEAKS, SAWATCH RANGE, CO

WE HAD BEEN WATCHING it closely after we had broken timberline. The storm moved in, with cheerless, thick clouds—like slow-moving waves spilling onto distant shores—swelling over the mountains west of us, and coming our way. Most of the terrain was lower than us at this point. The clouds became darker as the storm drew closer. We tried to evaluate our situation and make a wise decision as how next to proceed.

After discussion, my brother-in-law, Kevin, and I still thought we could top our second 14,000-ft. peak of the day and get down before the tempest hit. Just dumb. It's exactly that kind of poor judgment that hikers have on these mammoth mountains before removing themselves from this life. Or bad choices like that can force Search and Rescue teams to put themselves in dangerous situations to try to find and drag your froze rear end off the mountain. I guide hikers up 14ers, and warn against challenging the elements. Nature always wins.

The storm surge rose toward us as we foolishly pressed on.

Okay, look, do as I say, not as I do. And let this be a cautionary tale.

We hadn't planned to climb two of Colorado's fourteeners that day, but we had an early start up Mount Harvard (14,423 ft.), and a warm, sunny sky greeted us (with an unnoticed wink). I guess we kind of forgot that even in the best of conditions in the Rockies, it's said that it's never summer above 12,000 feet.

Having topped Harvard, and now with the summit of neighboring Mount Columbia within our grasp, we were slammed by an absolute whiteout in August. What at one point looked still so far away, was now on top of us. It all happened so fast. Horizontal blowing snow stung our faces and reduced visibility to zero. The temperature dropped 30 degrees. The blizzard surrounded us with no escape. We weren't going up any higher, and we could not easily descend over the now slippery, snow-covered rocks. The best we could do was to find a place to hunker down and ride out this maelstrom.

Kevin pointed to some vaguely silhouetted boulder piles to our left. We struggled against the wind to find some shelter. We both crawled into tight spaces about 10 yards from each other, our backs against the cold rock.

Having well-stocked backpacks, we pulled everything out quickly and put on all the extra clothes we had, plus gloves, knit caps and rain ponchos. Blowing snow collected over my hiking boots that were exposed outside of my shallow cave. We waited. And waited. And shivered uncontrollably.

We recognized the first stages of hypothermia. I yelled through the din to Kevin to compare notes through frozen lips. He concurred about the danger of our circumstances, I think. His muffled voice may have shouted a question about whose stupid idea was this. I wasn't going to volunteer or accuse.

We had to do something. It was obvious that this weather system wasn't moving away any time soon. This wasn't one of those 15-minute Colorado summer afternoon rain storms. This was like a winter snowstorm. We made the decision to try and head down. Out of our holes, I looked up, or at what should have been up. It was only a half mile or so to the top, there somewhere. It surprised me that Kevin agreed to my suggestion that we make a blast for the summit. It was so close, after all. This is another poor decision hikers make that sends rescuers after their broken bodies at the base of a cliff, a look of combined confusion and regret on the hikers motionless faces.

After a few clumsy, stutter-steps upward, right thinking got the better of us. We chose to live and climb another day. The mountain would still be there when we returned. Carefully, over icy, slick rocks, we worked our way back down. By the time we reached the forest, the snow had turned to rain. As if to punish us for our bad choices that day of an additional peak, under those inclement conditions, the storm dumped buckets of water on us all the back to our SUV. No mater how much you try to cover up, rain will find its way in somehow.

With, perhaps, a little too much ambition and enthusiasm, we had found ourselves in a challenging situation. Thankfully we were ready, did the right things (finally!), and made it out. Soaking wet, chilled, but safe. These are stories I don't like to have to tell Diane when I get home. She expects me to hike and climb smarter.

Chapter Ten
THE PEOPLE YOU MEET

"I have no idea what's going to happen. And I love it!"—Anonymous

MOUNT MANITOU INCLINE/BARR TRAIL, MANITOU SPRINGS, COLORADO

I OVERHEARD this conversation below on the Barr Trail on this hike:

"Why did you bring me up here again?! I told you I didn't want to come. I told you!" The young woman looked exhausted, and was clearly, and loudly, upset at her boyfriend or husband (if that relational status lasts).

"I thought you liked the Incline, the one time you climbed it before," he answered.

"I thought I did ... but I was wrong!"

I too have a love-hate relationship with the Mount Manitou Incline in Manitou Springs (and the connecting Barr Trail): I love to hate it, and I hate to love it. But I climb the Incline with hoards of other hikers pretending to love it. Hard to understand that this stair step old railway rail bed is one of the most climbed trails in Colorado, but it does give hikers sweeping views and is quite a fitness challenge.

The Manitou Incline Trail is the remains of a historic narrow gauge railway, a cable tram that began operation in 1907. The railway was originally constructed to provide access to a pipeline on top of the mountain that provided gravity-fed pressure to the hydroelectric plants of Manitou Springs and Colorado Springs. Soon after construction, the railway opened as a tourist attraction. The tracks were washed out in a rock slide in 1990.

I have done this brutal trail a number of times. From the trailhead, the Incline rises 2,000 feet in just about one mile, with an average grade of 45%, as steep as 68% in some places, and tops off at 8,590 feet. A number of summers ago, I was climbing the Incline three times a week with son-in-law Joe, trying to beat one hour to the top. By autumn, I finally summited at 58 minutes. Pretty good for my age. Nowhere near the U. S. Olympic Training Center athletes' time of 30 minutes or under, but then I'm no Olympic athlete. I was satisfied and haven't climbed it again.

This summer morning the sun shown brightly, a welcome relief after many days of our typical monsoon seasonal rain. Wispy clouds floated on a gentle breeze over the valley below. I chose to hike the adjacent Barr Trail for an above-the-incline exploration of nearly-hidden historical remnants (research for a book I was writing). I had hiked this long Barr Trail years earlier, the full 13.5 miles to the summit of Pikes Peak, taking a painstaking nine hours to reach the top.

I slowly huffed and puffed up what really is a very moderate 4-mile, well-maintained hiking trail with a turnoff spur to the top of the Manitou Incline. I paced myself with short rest and photo stops. Even with the many switchbacks, this was still a 2,000-ft elevation gain to my destination. The full-sized Cog Railway train's horn echoed in the canyon to my left as the engine departed the depot and started chugging up the mountain taking passengers to the Summit House on the top of Pikes Peak.

Continually, I had to step aside for what seemed like an endless flow of downhill runners—those having completed the climbing steps on the Incline—passing me like the wind, not even breathing hard. They were 10 yards beyond me by the time they responded to my "Good morning!" greeting. As I continued my ascent, a young woman flew by me going *uphill* like I was standing still, not hampered in the least by the large plastic boot on her foot from some serious ankle injury!

Many of the hikes and adventures I tell about in this book will take you to isolated, serene, get-away-from-the-crowds experiences. This is not one of those. There is a literal parade of hikers up and down the Barr Trail, at least until you reach the top of the Incline. If you enjoy people-watching, listening in (briefly, in passing) to others' exchanges, and like chatting with fellow hikers about your shared experience, then this adventure is still for you.

My first conversational encounter was with a red-faced, middle-aged woman who asked, "Is this the correct way down, to where I want to go?"

Now understand, I don't always say out loud what I'm thinking. This helps me not get slapped frequently in public, especially by strangers. So … I'm thinking: *How would I know—where is it you want to go? And you are up here with no researched plan as how to get down?* I do want to respond kindly to others needing help in the wilderness. Really. So, I simply said yes, and that the trail would take her down to the parking lot and then on to the Cog Railway Depot at the top of Ruxton Avenue. That seemed the way she wanted to go.

It was now mid-morning, as I had started the trail later than planned. I came upon two exhausted, heavily-perspiring young men sitting on boulders. I learned that they were from Illinois, and had never climbed a 14er before. I told them that a same-day summit of Pikes Peak (especially a 26-mile round trip climb) needed to have a pre-dawn start and a better pace than they were keeping, especially with the expected afternoon thunderstorms. I shared with them gruesome stories of those struck by lightning on Colorado mountains above treeline, including on Pikes Peak. They agreed with my strong suggestion that they spend the night at Barr Camp halfway up the trail. They would summit in the morning. I may have just saved two lives.

I continued on up the trail. I don't deliberately listen into other folks' private conversations (most of the time) but on a crowded mountain trail, many hikers seem to have no self-awareness of others passing by, or how voices carry farther in thin air.

Two 20-something women: "I'm going to have to lie, aren't I? Am I going to have to lie?"

Two pimply-faced teen girls: "If she could just get rid of that acne, she could look pretty good."

One woman to another: "I hate it when they throw up on me, don't you?" I don't even want to know the backstory on that one. I hope she was talking about infants!

Older man sitting on log: "Real men take rest stops!"

A boy to his parents: "I am *never* climbing that again! Never, ever."

Bright-pink, overweight man (obviously teasing with those that passed him): "So glad I was able to do the Incline in under 30 minutes!"

Right, Olympic athlete pace. Uh, huh.

Not to be outdone, I shouted out with a smile, "I'm on my *third* round-trip today!"

My first encounter with the next group coming down together was a bare-chested man in a kilt running with a huge American flag on a long pole. That's certainly not something one sees everyday on a mountain trail. I concentrated on the flag as he passed and not on the wildly flapping kilt. I was going to thank him for his patriotism, but he quickly rounded a turn and was gone.

Others soon passed, obviously associated by their comradery, somber spirit, and in most cases, matching apparel. I was now nearing the top of the Incline, having followed the connecting trail from the Barr Trail. Some had flags draped over their shoulders. A couple carried the large oxygen tanks used by rescue workers. Some had firefighter uniforms attached to their backpacks. At the top, it now made sense what this group was all about. Many that were departing to join the others wore the heavy fireman's protective jackets and pants and full gear.

I chatted with a couple of the men and found out that they were from the local Cheyenne Mountain Fire Department. They had climbed the Incline this day—one month and one day early, due to an upcoming closure for more trail improvements—to pay tribute to the 343 firefighters who lost their lives on 9-11. I found out that similar hikes are done all over the country each year to honor the fallen.

One said, "We chose the Incline because, with its 2,000 stairs to the top, this is the best resemblance to the World Trade Center in our area."

Another stated, "We are here to carry on their legacy ... a memorial for our lost brothers and sisters, and for the family members." I thanked them for doing this, and for their service to our community.

Above the Incline, I sat on the old concrete foundation of all that's left of the original hoist house that powered the single cable for the two railway cars. I could still see the mounting for the machinery. I had some trail snacks and gulped down water as I watched hikers reach the top of the steps, both exhausted and exhilarated. Hoots and hollers and hugs and high-fives followed.

I spent the hour or so exploring around the top for historical remnants of times when tourists rode the train to the summit house in the early1900s. My friend (and co-writer of the upcoming book on easy hikes to the hidden past), Rocky Shockley, had provided me with a list of relics to look for on this exploration, and a diagram to follow—a historical artifact treasure map, if you will. Some things were very evident; others were hard to find and took some Indiana Jones-style searching to make the discoveries. My exploration did feel like a treasure hunt, but for treasured recollections of times mostly forgotten, of items and buildings constructed for a purpose, their usefulness long passed, and of lives lived in and around these lost objects from the past. Unlike a treasure hunt for riches however, I took away wonderful memories, golden moments reflecting on what life must have looked like on top of Mount Manitou back in the day.

I imagined the men and women in the early 1900s riding the Incline train to the top, with a similar breeze as today blowing across the open box cars. I saw myself meeting some of them, just as I might today at the summit. In the past, all of the women are in dresses; all the men in suits and ties. All have hats on—both the men and the women—and they look like they are going to some evening social event, not a wilderness adventure.

As if they had come back to life, in my mind's eye, I saw the visitors disembark, stretch their legs, adjust their hats, and look down on jaw-dropping views of Manitou Springs, on to Colorado Springs and the prairie lands to the east beyond, just as the Incline stair climbers do today. A few of the historic train riders still wore a grimaced look on their faces from what must have been a harrowing trip up the steep mountain side. They were probably also considering the ride back down.

Some of the guests from bygone days now make their way to the snack bar and gift shop. A number had brought their own wicker baskets and wander over to the picnic tables made from iron train rails. Others hike up to Eagles Point to take in the views of Ute Pass to the north. A few of the more hearty walk on a bit farther to get an extraordinary view of Pikes Peak through the pines.

I continued my hunt for remnant objects from the past (I even found some artifacts not on Rocky's list!). I came upon a hiker returning down from the Barr Trail back to the top of the Incline. He must have seen my note papers, pen and the explorer's determination in the search.

"Find anything interesting up here?" he inquired. "Any hidden treasures?"

I smiled. Well, as a matter of fact ....

I was curious to venture on another half mile upward to where I was reconnected to the Barr Trail. From here I could continue a short distance farther to the foundation remains and stairs of buildings from the early 20th century Manitou Experimental Forest project. This was an attempt to determine what type of other planted trees could exist at this elevation. It should come as no surprise that only the native trees can be seen today.

Sunlight and shadow moved in waves across the green grass between and around the ruins. I looked up to see clouds growing in varying hues of grays. I should have gotten an earlier start to my hike. It was time to head back down the mountain. My explorations were over, but my day of meeting people on the trail was not yet done.

Descending the Barr Trail again I came upon a rather distraught looking woman and her young daughter. Two good-sized backpacks lay on the ground just off the trail. She was having what appeared to be a very panicky conversation on her cell phone. I stopped to see if I could be of any assistance.

"My husband went to look for my lost son," she said with a lot of emotion in her voice. "He ran ahead of us after the top of the Incline."

I leant a listening ear to a very upset mom and learned that her 12-year old (who apparently knew *exactly* where he was going, and didn't want to wait for the rest of the family) took off and quickly marched out of sight of his parents, despite their pleas for him to slow down and stay together. Mom was on the phone with her now equally upset son, both trying to determine his unknown location. The woman explained that her husband backtracked to try to find Junior. She didn't know where either of them were now. I offered my help for the search.

After a few minutes, Dad returned from a side trail to the spot where Mom stood, still trying to steer Junior towards her. The problem was that neither she nor he knew where the other one was located. Dad told me that the lost pathfinder must have taken the connecting trail from the Incline to the Barr Trail, and turned down instead of up, the way they were suppose to go toward their camping spot by the Experimental Forest. The three fourths of the family felt they should now stay put, rather than separating and taking the chance of missing him on the trail. I told them I was heading down the Barr Trail and that I would see if I could find the young lad and send him up the trail to them. I asked for a description of the boy, which I was given, one that included a bright green day pack. Thunder clapped in the distance. I knew I had to move, for myself and for this family.

What had grown as thick, angry clouds over Pikes Peak, now covered the whole region like a gray blanket. The once distant thunder was a lot closer. I quickened my pace. I was a bit nervous, and imagined what the young boy was feeling.

Around a turn in the trail, a middle-aged man waved me

over. "Do you know a good place for lightning, on the mountain?"

Oooooh-kay…

Knowing his meaning, I still responded, "Yes, pretty much *anywhere* on the mountain is a good place for lightning."

" I mean—"

I helped him. "You mean, where is a good place to hide from lightning on a mountain?

"Yes."

"Nowhere."

I told him how I'd seen trees in the middle of the forest split down the center by lightning. How I'd come upon burnt-out corpses of trunks in open spaces. I shared that at the Devil's Playground on the Pikes Peak Highway, crazy visitors will sit in their cars at the parking area in a thunderstorm, and will watch the lightning jump from rock to rock. And I explained that thunder and lightning doesn't have to be right above you to be dangerous. Lightning can travel 20 miles and make a strike. There is nowhere to hide from lightning in a severe weather conditions. The best option is to just get down to lower elevations right away, actually running sometimes. I suggested that he should head back to the trailhead, and pronto. I proceeded down, but didn't know if he followed.

About three miles from the parking lot, a lone boy with a bright green pack walked slowly uphill, talking on a cell phone. He had an expression of disorientation and worry on his face, but otherwise looked no worse for the wear. This was about a mile from where I had left his family. I cautiously greeted him (not wanting to be *that* creepy guy on a wilderness trail) and explained that I had met with his parents and would look for him down the trail.

I asked if I could talk to his mom on the phone. He seemed surprised at the request, but handed it over to me. I told Mom that her son was okay, and that I would send him up the trail. She sounded so relieved and thanked me. I gave the young fella the phone back along with clear directions to take him back to his folks.

"What did we learn from this experience?" I asked with a sing-song wink in my voice.

"Not to run ahead … and become separated from the group."

We had a "high-five." He seemed embarrassed, but relieved at the same time. My work here was done.

A light drizzle started. I pulled out my rain poncho. In another half an hour, it started to rain hard. And it rained. And it rained some more. The path down became slick and muddy, with some areas looking more like a stream than a trail. I came upon descending others who took cover under large boulders or trees. Then, just as fast as the storm began, the rain passed through and the sun warmed me out on my poncho.

By this time, I neared the trailhead and parking lot. My hike was almost complete, but my day of meeting people was not yet done. I first saw the slow-walking woman from a distance. As I drew nearer, I couldn't believe what I saw. It looked like she was trail hiking and smoking! And it wasn't Colorado's loco weed.

Who hikes and smokes?

Understand, I'm not judging. It's just that the two simultaneous activities seem so incongruous. Hard to see how it's really possible, in the thin air, and with strenuous exercise.

I had seen this once before, on another 14er, at the completion of the summit. A man with a stoma in his neck (a surgical hole to allow air to go in and out of the trachea) arrived on top and sat down on a flat rock. Boy, I had to give him credit for climbing a peak with is obvious physical challenges. Almost immediately, the poor fellow lights up and sticks the cigarette right into the hole to take a deep inhale of tobacco! It was a nightmarish image I'll never forget.

I moved up to pass Smoking Woman. To my surprise, what she held in her hand was not a lit cigarette, but simply a white ballpoint pen. She looked to be journaling her experiences on the mountain just like I had been.

Of course, I had to stop and tell her of my misinterpreted impression. She laughed, but then went on to tell of her quite inspirational story. She thought it was funny and ironic that I saw what I thought I saw.

"Actually, I could never have done a hike like this up to two years ago ... could never have done the Incline," Liz said.

Emotion slowed her speech. Regaining composer, she went on to share that she had been a heavy smoker for 18 years. Afraid she'd not be around for her kids and grandkids, one day she stopped smoking cold turkey and never again picked up a coffin nail. Committed to a healthier lifestyle, she began eating better and started running as well. She lost 40 pounds. As proof of better choices, she was determined to climb the Manitou Incline. Today was that day. I congratulated her for her accomplishment, and told her I was happy to hear her story and so pleased about her personal victory.

I love hiking and exploring. I often solo hike and enjoy the quiet and serenity of the wilderness. But, sometimes part of the adventure can be in the discovery of those you meet along the way. I had no idea when I started this hike what, or who, I'd encounter. I love how it turned out.

Chapter Eleven

LOST AT LOST LAKES

"I'm not lost, I'm exploring."—Author unknown (perhaps never found)

LOST LAKES LOOP TRAIL, FLAT TOPS WILDERNESS, COLORADO

My "bucket list" of must-do trail hikes is turning into a short list. Either I've done many of them or realize I'm running out of time, and I have had to trim the checklist down. At my age, I'm grateful that I've still got good knees, hips, shoulders, feet, back, and eyesight—better than most of my friends. I'm fortunate, and thank God for the blessing of good health. But I'm not getting any younger. I can still do the long hikes, but a thru-hike on the 2,200-mile Appalachian Trail is probably off the table.

One hike that Kevin and I have wanted to do for years is the Lost Lakes Loop Trail in the Flat Tops Wilderness in northern Colorado. This 19.5-mile hike that we did as a day hike (most would backpack 2-3 days), is outside Steamboat Springs in a 235,406-acre designated wilderness area and, if you choose, ends with the infamous Devil's Causeway. The causeway portion of this adventure is at 11,800 feet and is just three feet wide in places. With sheer drops of several hundred feet, this challenge is not for those prone to vertigo. Some say that nearly everyone who attempts the crossing is quite literally brought to his or her knees, scrambling across the rocky path in a low squat. We had been in worse places.

Allow me to pause and ponder something: Why are so many sightseeing locations named for the devil? We've got Devil's Tower, Devil's Postpile, Devil's Lake, Devil's Golf Course, Devil's Thumb, and more. Either the devil has a huge ego (which I imagine he does) or we just like to name unusual, scary, or creepy natural wonders after Lucifer. May I suggest to the chambers of commerce near these locations that they consider more friendly names to increase tourist traffic? Something that replaces the word *devil* with titles like *bunny, kitten, ice cream, dove,* or *pillow.* Certainly families would flock to see Rock Candy Arch, Marshmallow Dunes or Puppy Island! But then, now that I think about it, places like Devil's Causeway are really not for children, so this name should probably stay.

One mid-summer, Kevin and I started up the Lost Lakes Trail above Stillwater Reservoir just after dawn, welcomed by a crisp, cloudless sunrise. The first mile and a half of the trail was quite steep but opened up fabulous views of the Flat Tops Wilderness. Established in 1975, it is the second largest wilderness area in Colorado. We passed through meadows of waist-high wildflowers and reached a saddle at 11,600 feet. A strong, cool breeze forced me to put on my lightweight windbreaker. From here, the trail dropped into a drainage and meandered through spruce and fir forests, open grassy parks and lichen-covered boulder fields.

If I had to limit myself to just one word describe this trail hike, I would say it was *epic.* I know that is overused, but it certainly applies to this adventure. The scenery in every direction revealed why I had this trip on my must-do list. I knew I was experiencing something very special, maybe a once-in-a-lifetime event.

The lost lakes were found—not too hard, as here the trail was well marked and took us shore side of still waters that reflected the azure sky, tall dark pines, and gathering puffy clouds. We passed Causeway Lake, Round Lake, Long Lake, Lost Lake, Deep Lake, and more lakes and ponds too numerous to list—

many not even named. (May I suggest Panda Lake for one? Everyone loves pandas ... more than devils.) I have never seen so many pristine lakes in one area. I took over 300 photos on this hike! Thank goodness for digital photography. I couldn't help myself. Kevin might have been annoyed at my slow, mouth-agape pace. We did want to get back to the SUV before dark. Shadowy shapes continually moved across the landscape as clouds passed over head.

If there was any downside to this wonderful experience, it was that in the shady areas of the valley we dropped down to, we got attacked by swarms of mosquitos, sometimes as thick as fog. I don't usually see much of these Devil Bugs (yes, I used that word here, deliberately and appropriately applied) on my hiking in Colorado, especially at the higher elevations. This time, I became a magnet for the bloodsuckers. They came in waves, each dive bombing and driving it's pointy proboscis deep into me. My only chance of escape was to try to outrun them back into the sunshine, where I hoped they would burn up in the light like the tiny vampires they are.

At around 2:30 in the afternoon, after ascending and breaking tree line again, we were lost. The Lost Lakes Trail was supposed to hit the junction of the Chinese Wall Trail ... according to the guidebook. Right. According to the book. But the book gave confusing and contradictory instructions. Had the writer/editor even been on this part of the trail?

Concerning times like this, I tell my wife, when I return safely, that I wasn't really lost. (I don't want her to worry.) Kevin and I knew exactly where we were. We had maps, GPS, a compass, experience and reasonable thinking. We weren't lost. We just didn't know where the trail was. Diane doesn't buy the distinction.

The book "expert" took us up the nearly 12,000-ft. Lost Lakes Peak, only to have the trail disappear off the top. Clearly we had made a wrong turn somewhere. It took us almost two hours and about two extra miles (beyond the 19.5) as we retraced our path and looked for the right turnoff. After we found where we had gone off course, the real work began. We trekked our way across high alpine tundra where most of the trail was faint or nonexistent. We had to "connect the dots" by keeping a good eye out for widely spaced rock cairn piles and trail posts. These tall stacked stones were probably spread out a half-mile apart, almost requiring binoculars to locate.

It was late in the day now, time lost from my picture-taking stops, removing our boots to ford snowmelt creeks, and trail reconnoitering to get back on track. We had six miles to cross at exposed elevation. Mercifully, the building clouds didn't dump on us. We had to keep moving, even though we were both exhausted. We did not want to have to cross the dreaded Devil's Causeway in the dark.

We hit the causeway portion of the trail with just moments to spare before sunset. We hurried to get the last of our journey photographed—especially crossing the three-foot wide section with 1,500 ft. drop-offs on each side—before dusk turned to orange-red then dark gray. Halfway across the narrow passage, we bid the sun good night. We still had miles to go back to the SUV.

With headlamps on, flashlights out, we shambled into the parking lot at 10:15, dog-tired, walking like old men (no surprise there). We had done it! One more bucket list hike checked off. Epic.

Chapter Twelve

THE SOUNDTRACK OF MY LIFE

"After silence, that which comes nearest to expressing the inexpressible is music."—Aldous Huxley, Music at Night and Other Essays

LOST LAKES LOOP TRAIL, FLAT TOPS WILDERNESS, COLORADO

For my hike on the Lost Lakes Loop, I did something that I've never done before: I brought music. On long-distance, remote, wilderness treks, I have always wanted to be alert to sounds of a predator looking for its next two-legged, trail-delivered meal.

I knew the Lost Lakes Trail was going to be a long day, so I thought I'd try something to get me through this endurance test. On my iPod were some movie soundtracks, instrumentals, Celtic choruses, and some Christmas music (why only around the holidays?). Okay, and I also have Classic Rock on the device, but that wasn't on the program for this hike.

I often "hit a wall" at about mile 12. I've had it. Long hikes are physically challenging, but just as much a mind game to keep going. Halfway around the loop, I pulled out my iPod and put in my ear buds. If a hungry mountain lion was going to get me, it was probably going to happen anyway, music or not.

This whole trail really is spectacularly beautiful. Beyond word description, really. I had already found countless lost lakes, been in thick forests, crossed streams by small waterfalls, and surveyed open meadows covered with an explosion of high alpine wildflowers.

I stood in a field, clicked on the iPod, and something unexpected and extraordinary happened. The music, starting with a sweeping instrumental, became like my soundtrack as I walked. It was a 360-degree **IMAX** theater experience, but live, not filmed. The peaceful music acted as background narration for what was unfolding all around me. The music did help me finish, including the last few miles of one painful, exhausted step after another.

LATER, I GOT TO WONDERING WHAT SORT OF SOUNDTRACK IS playing in the background in my everyday life, far from the mountains. If I viewed my work-a-day world as a film, would I hear loud and chaotic music, shouting in my head? I have a feeling I know the answer to this question: Many times the "music" is like screeching, dissonant violins in a horror movie! Perhaps it's time to bring some of the wilderness tranquility to my day-to-day living.

The lions in life might still hunt me; I'll still be looking over my shoulder. But, hopefully, I'll go down with serenity and a smile.

Chapter Thirteen

SLIP HAPPENS

"I don't know why it is we are in such a hurry to get up when we fall down. You might think we would lie there and rest for a while."—Max Eastman

BEAR LAKE, ROCKY MOUNTAIN NATIONAL PARK, COLORADO

It was supposed to be such a simple, relatively-easy snowshoe hike, the first big hike of that calendar year for me. The past three months of that winter had been complicated, and I wasn't able to get outside much. That always makes me a bit crazy. I mean more than usual.

I had snowshoed to these three high-alpine frozen lakes in Rocky Mountain National Park a few winters prior, looked forward to the familiar spectacular beauty, and felt the hike itself would be fairly routine. I needed some scenic winter photos for my annual calendar, and I knew this mountain setting would deliver. I couldn't have known this trip would turn out to be a comedy of errors—that is, if you find these kinds of things funny. You know, cruelly laughing at the misfortunes of others.

My two-and-a-half hour drive to the park started before dawn. Nothing unusual there. I frequently start my hiking days early. I got my typical wake-up cup of java on the way, and an energy-producing breakfast, chased with an orange juice. I don't know what happened, what got me, but when I arrived at the Visitor Center, I had to run to the restroom anticipating the BIG D, with explosive results. My apologies to you for having to read this. My apologies to the custodial staff at the Visitor Center. This wasn't how a hiking day was suppose to start, and I especially didn't want to have similar lower intestinal events on the trail.

Shortly, I began to feel better and drove to the entrance to pay my fee. I used my standard joke at the booth, asking if it's okay to approach and feed the wild animals. It always gets a chuckle, even if it's only by me. I did tell the good-humored park ranger about my plans (but not about the restroom) and inquired about snow levels and trail conditions. He said I could expect a good snowshoe hike but advised me to stay off the lakes as they were starting to thaw around the edges. Also, he warned me that if I proceeded past the third lake to higher slopes, I could be in avalanche danger. I vowed to follow his instructions. I always enjoy a good day out winter hiking that doesn't involve falling into icy hypothermia-inducing waters or getting clobbered and buried by a freight train of cascading snow.

I got to the trailhead parking lot at Bear Lake well ahead of other weekend hikers. I stuffed extra T. P. in my backpack, just in case. I put on my heavily insulated boots and my gaiters, and grabbed my hiking stick with a snow basket foot. I also secured my snowshoes on my pack with a bungee cord. Since the trail began with a mix of snow, exposed dirt, and rock, I had decided to wait before putting on my snowshoes, with their nice ice-grabbing teeth, until I was farther up the trail where the snow got deeper. Clearly a rookie mistake, and I am no rookie. I was now feeling surprisingly well, considering my start, excited for my day's adventure.

Not twenty yards from the parking lot, I slipped on an ice patch and came down hard on my rear end (yes, *that* rear end), and bent my wrist back with stinging pain, as I tried to break my fall. *Seriously?* I hadn't even *started* the hike yet!

Flat on my back, hoping no one had seen me go down (being

the experienced hiker and all, with the right clothing and equipment), I stayed put for a few moments, looking like an overturned turtle, and took injury assessment. Thankfully, my pack had taken the brunt of the fall, but my wrist hurt like a son-of-a-gun.

Probably just a sprain, I thought, *hopefully nothing worse.* I considered that I might just lie there for a short while, and rest. But my humiliation hurt more than my arm, and other hikers were coming up from the parking lot. I slid down the short, slippery stretch, rolled a couple times, and carefully got back to my feet.

Undaunted, I dug into my well-stocked pack. I found my medical supply bag, wrapped my throbbing wrist with an Ace bandage, strapped my snowshoes onto my boots, and started up the steep valley. I was here for a purpose, and no way was I going back without my calendar photos!

The scenery did not disappoint as I passed by (but not across) Nymph Lake on my way to Dream Lake, both still frozen over but slushy around the edges. I looked up through the pines at a deep blue sky that can be seen in such a rich tone only at high altitude. Enthralled at the beauty of the dappled light through the forest on the its snowy carpet, I wasn't too bothered by continually trying to refasten my pack belt buckle ... until I was *terribly annoyed* at it endlessly popping open.

Apparently, as a result of my fall, not only had I possibly broken my arm, but I had definitely broken my plastic pack buckle with the impact on the small ice rink. Without the security of the belt for stability and proper weight distribution, the flopping pack was making me quite uncomfortable. I tried tying the belt around my waist with poor results. Somehow, I'd make the best of it.

As I approached the egress of Dream Lake, the belt popped open again. My attached camera pouch fell away as well, and because I hadn't properly zipped the bag shut, out tumbled my camera. I watched in slow motion as it bounced away from me on another ice patch. *Nooooo!* I had come all this way for scenic snow shots, and I looked in horror as my camera came to rest inches from an icy stream.

My stomach gurgled. Great. Not now, please. Not here. Picking up the camera, I could not see any obvious lens or body damage. I tested it from a location that gave me an iconic shot across a lake encircled by pines, with jagged snow capped peaks in the background. The camera worked and I got my shot! I used a bungee cord as a pack belt— as stupid as that may have looked —by attaching it to parts of the pack, and continued on to Emerald Lake.

The Emerald Lake bowl was breathtaking, although the now white lake itself not too emerald this time of year. I enjoyed a snack lunch sitting in warm sun on boulders above the lake. "Camp robber" birds begged for treats from pine boughs an arm's distance away. I watched back-country skiers (obviously having ignored the warning from the park ranger) struggling up snow slopes on the other side of the lake with their skis covered in "skins" for grip. I needed to head back, so I didn't have time to wait and watch the avalanche bash and tumble the skiers to their doom.

On my way back. I realized again that the trail conditions were less than ideal in places for snowshoeing. Fresh snow had not fallen in days, it was packed down in places from other hikers, and in sections the warmth of the day had melted the snow, only to refreeze at night, making early morning hikes a bit challenging. So, even with the snowshoe teeth grabbing what they could, I fell a few times. In truth, on hikes, especially on mountain climbs, I fall a lot. It's embarrassing. Nothing too serious, I mean not deadly falls. I consider it all part of the experience, like a badge of honor, coming down off a 14,000-ft. peak, and slipping on scree.

I had a great hike this day, even with the unexpected challenges and a painful wrist. In some ways it was better because on the trials. I got the photos I was after. And one never knows how a routine hike may actually turn into a story. You can't make *wilde*rnes memories without actually getting out there. The rewards far outweigh the risks; you might just slip into a great adventure.

Chapter Fourteen

THE MONASTERY

"Curiosity will conquer fear even more than bravery will."—James Stevens

MATER DOLOROSA PASSIONATE RETREAT CENTER, SIERRA MADRE, CALIFORNIA

WE CREPT around the grounds of the retreat center like it was secret government facility. We stayed behind trees, in the shadows. If caught, we knew we'd spend weeks to months to years in some kind of cloistered, wayward-children's jail, cuffed and chained against a dank stone wall, deep in a dark basement. Or, at the very least, we thought, we'll be chased down by guard dogs, grabbed by the collar by some very athletic monks in robes and Adidas running shoes, and then have our knuckles rapped with a ruler.

For an adventurous and curious boy growing up in Sierra Madre, California, the acreage and the buildings were always a mystery, and, well, needed to be explored—even if in a clandestine manner. The official name of the 83-acre property set on the piedmont of the San Gabriel Mountains is Mater Dolorosa Passionate Retreat Center (originally called Monte Olivette), but we always referred to it simply as the Monastery.

We could look down on the grounds when my young friends

and I hiked around the surrounding foothills. The property really sat adjacent to the trailhead access of Bailey Canyon. This is the canyon where I had many wonderful childhood adventures. Years later I took my own kids up to explore the ravine into the mountains, climb boulders, and swim in the cool water of an eddy in the stream.

When my boyhood friends and I explored the Monastery, trying to uncover the mysteries hidden to us, we had no idea at the time that the retreat center housed permanent residents, as well as hosting men's retreats and others visiting for spiritual solace. We just knew that there was "something going on in there."

I had a good friend who lived right near the property gates on Sunnyside Street. This was a fine launch pad for our Hardy Boys investigation. We'd pack snacks into our canvas book packs intending to explore until our curiosities were satisfied.

We would actually end up spending very little time sneaking around the housing, the Stations of the Cross, or the olive garden, since one of us would quickly chicken out and we'd all bolt, thinking spying eyes were actually upon us in return. We feared that the occupants had alerted security, and black sedans were racing our direction, driven by hooded friars with sunglasses and walkie-talkies.

Of course, nothing could have been further from the truth. I'm sure that if we had just asked, the loving, peaceful, tranquil residents would have been more than happy to give some inquisitive boys a tour. The thing is, we never *saw* anyone, ever. When we got close to buildings, we may have heard muffled noises from the interior, but I think we convinced ourselves that it was playback from a reel-to-reel recorder, volume turned up to large speakers to make us think someone was home.

When we gathered up our bravery to return, if we were ever seen creeping around, we were never chased out. Most likely we were just ignored by those who lived there, perhaps with a smile … and maybe a wink to one another, remembering their own boyhood adventures.

Chapter Fifteen
WILDERNESS ANARCHY

"I believe in rules. Sure I do. If there weren't any rules, how could I break them?"—Leo Durocher

TABEGUACHE PEAK AND MOUNT SHAVANO, SAWATCH MOUNTAIN RANGE, CO

HIKING and climbing books typically have their lists of dos and don'ts for trail etiquette, safety and enjoyment. These "rules" are meant to enhance your time and that of others in the outdoors. They can also help get you out of the forest or down the mountain alive and in one piece. For the most part, I've been a law-abiding, wilderness citizen.

I've compiled my own "Ten Commandments for Hiking" (based on generally accepted hiking principles):

1. Stay on the trail.
2. Know the regulations, permit requirements, private property boundaries and any special concerns for the area you are visiting.
3. Treat our national, natural heritage with respect. (Oh course, it goes without saying, pack your trash out, leaving no trace.)
4. Come prepared for any circumstance.

5. Never, ever leave your pack.
6. Drink a lot of water (hydration) and eat energy snacks (fuel).
7. Dress in layers—you can always peel off clothing for comfort.
8. Be aware of your environment and climate conditions; constantly watch the sky for changes in the weather.
9. Spend money on good hiking shoes or boots—one of the best investments you can make.
10. Take care of "hot spots" on feet before they become blisters.

I can't say with a straight face that I have always lived by my own set of rules. I've got some stories in my book, *Tales from the Trails*, that show how I found myself and others in trouble when I didn't follow my guidelines. The phrase "Rules are made to be broken" may be true in some contexts. But in the untamed, unforgiving high country, wilderness anarchists can get themselves killed.

I might add a Number 11 to my commandments list: *Be smart and flexible.* There's a fine line between determination and stupidity. We need to use our heads and make good choices. I know from some of the stories I tell of my wilderness adventures that on this point I may sound like a hypocrite. It's a fine line at times, and a judgment call other times. Storm clouds might change direction and the day become warm and sunny again. You might easily negotiate yourself out of feeling lost. You might be able to take care of a hot spot or bad blister and be able to press on. But, we need to be willing to turn around at times if we have to. If the weather turns sour or dangerous, if you can't find the right path, if your conditioning is not up to the challenge, come back and try another day.

The "rules" for the trail are not intended to be constraining but are there to protect us, to safeguard the environment and to make our overall experience a good one. Plus they keep us from being stupid. Children (and I don't mean to imply they are stupid), especially, love to "trail blaze" off the main path. A little bit of this fun exploration can be an interesting diversion for them and add to the memories of the day—climbing on a boulder, peeking under a log for a bug community, catching an off-trail panoramic canyon view, or taking a short detour to see a gurgling creek or a scenic waterfall.

I stay (mostly) on the trail so that, except for the path, the rest of the environment is kept in as pristine condition as possible. That way the next hiker can have the same experience I've had. Shortcutting breaks up the natural look and can lead to erosion. Flattened wildflowers, broken branches, overturned logs or stones, disturbed wildlife, and moss or tundra damage do not show care for nature or respect to fellow hikers. One hiker or family going off trail may not make that big of an impact, but what if everyone did it?

Fragile ground plants carpeting the mountainside above timberline are especially vulnerable as they cling to a tenuous existence. If a misplaced step destroys a patch of alpine tundra in this delicate ecosystem, it may take decades for the plants to recover, if ever.

Another reason I stay on the prescribed path is so I don't get lost. This may sound very basic, but departing from the trail and improvising can put you in real trouble. I have gotten myself lost, or in a precarious position, and I don't care for it. Experienced others have gone before you to determine the safest, easiest and most direct route to your destination. You'd think I would learn this lesson.

I climbed Colorado's Tabeguache Peak (14,162 ft.) in combination with an accent up Mount Shavano (14,231 ft.)—Shavano being my second summit of the day. It's not a particularly hard climb compared to many others. But as a combination of two 14ers, it does make for a longer day. And the standard route requires the climber to summit Tabeguache twice! Up Tabeguache, down to a saddle between the two peaks, then up to the top of Mount Shavano—only to have to backtrack and climb over Tabeguache again. It is like climbing *three* 14ers in one day.

On the standard route, a hiker (a stupid one, that is—I speak from experience) is tempted to second-guess the book instructions and try to find a shortcut to save time and reduce some wear and tear on the legs. Or to find a way off the top quickly if a storm is fast approaching. It is never worth it.

On mountains, one drainage can look like the next, another canyon like the last. It's easy to get disoriented. Any attempt to find an "easier" route down off these two peaks can actually work against your objectives. Descending down one wrong gulch can ambush you with dangerous cliffs. Coming down another wrong canyon will leave you miles from your trailhead and car. Believe me, I know.

On Tabeguache Peak, I broke my Commandment No. 1: I strayed off the trail. Discouraged at having to put in the hard work of climbing up Tabeguache *again*, and tempted by an "easier" route, I decided to leave the main trail, intending to circumnavigate the peak instead of climbing up and over the top again.

I thought I could traverse around the peak, below the summit, saving time and effort, and meet back up with the main trail again. What a mistake! There was no path here, just acres of unstable talus. No rock could be trusted to support my weight or not move on me, creating real opportunities to twist an ankle, or worse. One rock would start to slide, gathering others, and suddenly I was riding a mini granite avalanche down hill.

My progress was slow and laborious. Sometimes I could step from rock to rock with trepidation, other times I'd test a rock only to discover that was not a step I wanted to pursue. I could navigate over some boulders by stepping up on others. But some were just too big and I had to go around, sometimes losing elevation that had to be made up again.

Once, a rock slipped out from under me and my leg disappeared into a small cave hole of stacked eroded debris. Fortunately, I went straight down, and wasn't carried by momentum to one side or the other. I scraped my leg up a bit, as well as my palm trying to arrest my fall. But, if I had broken my leg, I was too far in the back country to drag myself out. And being that I was the only one on those two mountains that day, there was no one to call to for help.

I did make it back to the trail—without serious injury— but

ended up saving no time and just made more work for myself. My reckless, revised route of choice was far more difficult and required dangerously negotiating over wobbly boulders, coming close to steep cliffs, and was simply exhausting, both in mind and body. Not to mention, it took me twice as long to complete.

So much for shortcuts … and breaking rules.

Chapter Sixteen
CREATURE DISCOMFORTS

"It ain't wilderness unless there's a critter out there that can kill you and eat you."—Doug Peacock

CLOUD CAMP, CHEYENNE MOUNTAIN, COLORADO SPRINGS

It had been a cold and snowy month. Thank you, El Niño. Or La Niña. I always get those two confused. I had cabin fever bigtime and desperately needed to get outdoors. I decided to do a short hike on Cheyenne Mountain in the Pike National Forest. The McNeil Trail is not well known, not well marked, and not well traveled. And it's directionally sketchy in places, especially with snow cover, with few cairns or other path indicators.

I had decided not to be too ambitious. I had some time constraints, hadn't been out hiking for a while, and was unfamiliar with the trail. It was just great to get some cool, fresh air and a bit of overdue exercise. I also had another agenda, just for fun. I wanted to see how many of the forest creature tracks in the fresh snow I could identify. I work for the Broadmoor Hotel in the winter, rotating through three wilderness camps as a property caretaker. It's a solo role, and at times, can be a little intimidating. I knew that in the off season, after the guests have departed, the wild beasties come back onto the properties. The previous year, one caretaker had lasted only one day, not just because he couldn't stand the isolation, but because he had seen mountain lion prints in the snow the size of coffee cup saucers on the lodge deck. Perhaps he was exaggerating. I had to see for myself.

The deeper I went into the woods, up and over a few ridges, moving from shadow to mid-day sunlight and back to pine cover again, the more tracks I saw. I do a fair amount of hiking year round, so I feel fairly confident about being able to recognize animal tracks. It is a little more difficult when they kick up powdered snow as they walk.

This day, some tracks were easy to identify, like rabbit, fox, perhaps a bobcat or lynx, even a hopping bird. Others were tougher, such as being able to differentiate a large deer from a small elk. One set of prints I simply had to guess. I came upon a literal freeway system of parallel and intersecting tracks.

I presume woodland critters are smart enough to take the path of least resistance through the forest, so they follow the hikers' trail, and other game trails. Sometimes the animal tracks overlap, making it hard to tell prints apart. One such print looked to me like some kind of weird hybrid between a bear and a gorilla. I laughed out loud! How utterly ridiculous—everyone knows bears are in hibernation this time of year, and the only gorillas close to the Rocky Mountains are in zoos!

As a sidebar, I did see actual bear tracks in the snow on the same road that I drive up to camp on the mountain. That surprised me. I thought they'd all be in deep-sleepy time. Upon further research, I discovered that our black bears in Colorado only *semi* hibernate! Turns out that if the weather warms up a bit one month, they may come out of their dens for awhile, only to return to go back to sleep again. My confidence that on a snowshoe hike, on a mild winter day, at least I wouldn't see a bear, was totally shattered!

I'm probably more worried about mountain lions. They will silently stalk you, quickly kill you with a neck clamp, eat you, and use your bones for a toothpick. At one of the other Broadmoor resort properties, Emerald Valley Ranch, on a couple of occasions, I have seen mountain lion paw prints in the snow. I never saw the feline predator, just the left evidence of a nocturnal visit. The large prints came up from the creek, went right by my caretaker cabin, and wound their way up past the stables where June Bug the barn cat lives year-round. She must be very resourceful, as she continues to survive, and greets me each morning, mewing for her breakfast.

Thankfully, on this Cheyenne Mountain hike, I didn't see any bear or mountain lion tracks. It was time to get back to the lodge. I had gone farther than I planned, and I had forgotten to bring a hiking stick, pepper spray and a small air horn. I had also forgotten my cell phone with the built-in camera. Out of hiking practice this time, I guess. You will have to take my word for it about the bear-gorilla-hybrid-creature footprints.

Chapter Seventeen
HEY, TAKE A HIKE!

"The more clearly we can focus our attention on the wonders and realities of the universe about us, the less taste we shall have for destruction."—Rachel Carson

SENTINEL POINT, 12,527 FT., PIKE NATIONAL FOREST, COLORADO

IT WOULD HAVE BEEN SO quiet in the forest, except for the woodland creatures greeting the dawn. Birds sang their morning songs and squirrels barked warnings of my arrival. Not bad noises in the woods. Soft light intermittently broke through the clouds and pine branches, stenciling the trail still wet from rain the previous night. The fir trees occasionally shared the mountainside with lime-green aspen groves, the leaves of which glistened moist in a light breeze.

The trail became more rugged and less distinct the higher I climbed. I found my way by connecting the dots of rock cairns. I continued upward, paralleling a bubbling brook. Cool water cascaded over small falls, sometimes coming to rest in tranquil pools. It was so peaceful here. I couldn't help but pause and think how crazy, unsettled, chaotic, and upside-down the world seemed at times. I felt so removed from all that noise and chaos as I sat for a time in the woods.

Sentinel Point stands guard on the west side of Pikes Peak.

After nearly four miles, I broke the tree line and continued up a rocky field to a large grassy saddle. To my right, a half mile away and still 500 feet higher, was my goal of the stacked boulder summit of Sentinel Point (12,500 feet), guarding the west slope of Pikes Peak on my left. For my effort, I was rewarded with jaw-dropping, 360-degree views.

Having scrambled to the top of the pile, I carefully turned a full circle. A Colorado spectrum blue sky met green velveted ridges dotted with red-tan boulders, some the size of camper trailers. Clouds alternately framed and blanketed Pikes Peak.

Black birds caught an updraft and floated by cliff edges. I breathed in slowly. It's hard not to be touched deep in your soul viewing a scene like this. Just wondrous.

Are you troubled? Stressed out? Worried? Take a hike.

Are you in need of calm? Quiet? Clarity? Take a hike.

I have to think, too, that if the chaos makers, the mean people, the haters, the arrogant, the condescending, the narcissistic, the angry folks on social media, the religious extremists, the terrorists, politicians, those with road rage, and the bullies would all just take a hike, it would do them a world of good. And it would make the world a better place.

Just go take a hike.

Chapter Eighteen
DETAILS COUNT

"Never put yourself in a position to be made an example of."—Gary Hopkins

COLORADO TRAIL, SEGMENTS 25 AND 26, SAN JUAN NATIONAL FOREST

I WAS EXHAUSTED, feet shuffling, head down. Just one more step, and one after that. That late fall, we had decided to do two connecting segments of the Colorado Trail over two days, covering 32 miles. Maybe we bit off more than we could trek. Not paying attention, I missed the cutoff trail back to our SUV. My bro-in-law, Kevin, was nowhere to be found.

Nothing looked familiar. The morning before—when we started out on the first segment—thick fog blanketed the mountains, blurring the forest, so I had no point of reference, except for a lake. *The* lake. Kevin had told me about this lake.

"Remember this lake. This will be the cut off tomorrow," he clearly said the day before. "When you see the lake, turn right, and take the spur trail down to the car."

Near the end of Day Two, I was convinced that Kevin couldn't have gotten that far ahead of me. We hike a lot together, so I know that he needs his space for writing (recording his next novel narrative), but I usually keep him in my sights.

Maybe *he* had taken a wrong turn and was MIA. Not me. I couldn't possibly be off track. I stayed my course, following the periodic triangular CT directional signs on the trees, connecting the dots on a continuing trail.

Dusk was settling in the shadows of these San Juan peaks. A bull elk bugled, quickly followed by frenzied howling from a pack of coyotes. I hoped they wouldn't turn their attention toward me! I felt lost but *was* still on the clear trail after all. How lost could I be? If I didn't get my bearings and connect with Kevin soon, I would be spending the night in the wilderness. I always pack prepared for such a possibility, but I would prefer not to have to bivouac on the side of a mountain.

Over an hour (and two more arduous miles) had passed since I last saw Kevin. I used my emergency whistle. Three blows, several times. Nothing. We had decided *not* to take our walkie-talkies, as we'd be hiking together this time, not coming toward each other from opposite trailheads as usual.

I had the idea to climb up to a high pass and try to use my cell phone, as crazy as that seemed, an act of desperation. No cell connection, but I decided to try to send Kevin a text describing my surrounding location, a large towering rock formation and compass-directional views. Surprisingly, there are occasions when a text can be sent and received in the wilderness. I wasn't going to hold my breath.

A moment later ... a return text! I couldn't believe it. Kevin knew exactly where I was by my description, and how I had gone wrong. What a relief!

"You can see Lizard Head Peak?" his text read. "You overshot the cutoff trail. You passed Celebration Lake, right?"

The lake! Yes! I had stopped for pics of the beautiful setting ... but completely missed the lake I was photographing. I was right there taking pics of the picturesque lake, and had completely missed the turn-off point. Too exhausted to pay proper attention, I guess.

Kevin had backtracked the trail when I was delayed, going back the way I had already passed, worried that I'd broken an ankle again or fallen off a cliff. Had he not gone to find me and entered a wide-open meadow, we wouldn't have received each other's texts. Texting each other in the wild—just crazy!

We followed the trail toward each other to meet up. It was great to see him—he may have been a little surprised by my enthusiastic, manly hug.

I'll be more alert to details (like an obvious lake) on our next hike!

Chapter Nineteen
THE TRAIL TO JUVENILE DELINQUENCY

"And now," cried Max, "let the wild rumpus start!"—Maurice Sendak, *Where the Wild Things Are*

SIERRA MADRE, FOOTHILLS, SAN GABRIEL MOUNTAINS, LOS ANGELES COUNTY, CALIFORNIA

I'VE ALWAYS BEEN one for an adventure, but I didn't always head out into the wilderness to find it. There were plenty of opportunities close to home when growing up in Sierra Madre, California.

This is a confession, and an apology, to many who resided in my little home town in the late 1960s to early '70s. Depending on what street you lived on, I may have:

- damaged your property,
- trespassed,
- disturbed your sleep,
- harassed your barking dog,
- stolen your morning newspaper,
- made prank calls (no caller I.D. in those days),
- egged or TPed your house or car,
- blown up your mailbox,

- menaced your younger children, and/or
- nearly given you a heart attack by exploding things in the street, making you think that the Cold War had accelerated to the real thing at the foothills of the San Gabriel Mountains, northeast of L.A.

And the list goes on.

It still amazes me that I'm not writing this chapter from prison. I wasn't *bad*; I just did bad things. My rationalization. I like to think that most of my aberrant boyhood behavior fell into the category of mischief-making rather than actual crimes (debatable, I suppose, where it came to trespassing and property damage). But had the pattern continued and escalated, I might today be looking at the world through steel bars, not through forest pine trees, and trying not to be my 300-pound cellmate's wife.

My friends and I took a rather lax view of the law, seeing it more as *suggestions*. It seemed like—in our young minds—that if you didn't get caught, and no one got hurt, then the act was permissible. I know, sounds like twisted logic and moral morass. I didn't get this graying of right and wrong from my parents (fine, upstanding community citizens)—I developed this worldview all by myself, well, along with that pesky peer influence. Admittedly, more of a nudge than actual pressure.

I liked to explode things. Sure, what boy doesn't, but my nearly-lawless friends and I took it to a new art and science. I could make accelerant and things that go boom out of many varied materials: matchstick heads, firecrackers, paint thinner, aerosols and something called Jetex that a kid could freely purchase at our local Toy and Patio Village in town. Jetex could be used to launch plastic rockets into Ray Bradbury cosmos ... but it was also handy to blow things up, if used just *wrong*. Other neighborhood junior mad scientists and I would build things just to explode them to pieces, sometimes right in the middle of the street.

Some of my friends had traveled to Tijuana, Mexico, south of San Diego, with their folks (did that make their parents accomplices?) and brought back cherry bombs and M-80s.

Someone told us that M-80s were the equivalent to a quarter stick of dynamite. True or not, we could blow things up real good with those! If, back in the day, you heard an ear-deafening explosion in your front yard and you came out to see your mailbox in pieces, I apologize. I think that if the federal government doesn't own mailboxes, it at least owns the space *inside*, so this may have been a federal crime. I trust the statute of limitations has run out on this.

One hot 4th of July picnic in Sierra Vista Park, by the wisteria vine-covered pergola below Heasly Field, a group of us explosives experts went up to the Little League field, detonation devices in hand. By each dugout there was a drinking fountain set in a large concrete pipe, half filled with small stones. Conceptually, this engineering was done for natural, slow drainage, but the cylinder barrel was always filled to the top with water. Someone (I'm not saying it was me) thought it would be fun to blast the water out of the fountain. Lighting and dropping a cherry bomb on the surface of the water produced a loud but unsatisfying result, splashing little water over the edge. So someone (okay, it was me) suggested that, with the fireproof fuse, we attach a weight to the next cherry bomb so it would sink down to the gravel at the bottom. This we did, and lit the fuse.

"Back up! Back up!" Several shouted. Good that we did.

The concussion was earsplitting and knocked us backwards. The explosion under pressure in the water sent a geyser 30 feet into the air. The concrete pipe crumbled into pieces. We were rained on and peppered with gravel. Mouths agape, we stared at the damage, our focus broken only by the screams and shouts from our parents running up from the picnic tables that were loaded with cold fried chicken, potato salad, chips, watermelon and soft drinks in ice buckets. All that remained of the fountain was a twisted freestanding water pipe.

Surprisingly, and fortunately, no one was hurt. All of us kids did have to share in the cost of a replacement fountain structure. We all were let off grounding to put in hours of community service for Little League field maintenance that included trash pickup, raking, weeding, painting and gopher control, eating up the valuable days of remaining summer fun. I think we had our bomb-making privileges taken away from us too, for a while.

I would like to say that incidences like this were life changing and put me on the path to reforming. But, alas, there were more wild misbehaviors I had to get out of my system, I guess. I'm sorry to those folks driving on Orange Grove Avenue at whom I threw firecrackers or spit peas through a straw. I feel bad for those cars on Baldwin Avenue that were splatted with water balloons from the cover of bushes. And for any inconveniences that my friends and I caused to neighbors and the Sierra Madre Volunteer Fire Department by setting small blazes in the middle of the street on Sunnyside, I apologize.

Residents of Sierra Madre, please forgive me for swimming in your drinking water. On many occasions, my friends and I would scale the chain link fences at the reservoirs above the baseball fields, strip down to our undies, and go for a refreshing summer swim. Why we didn't just go to the Sierra Madre Community Swimming Pool, not far from the reservoirs, I don't know. Maybe because that cost something, or because trespassing and plunging into a forbidden place was just more exciting.

I'm sorry if on a Sunday morning your fat *L. A. Times* newspaper came up missing, taken for the color comics. I'm sorry if you had to chase me and my friends (or enemies) off your grove property, after having been engaged in an all-out war of orange salvos. I feel bad that we would call Robert's Market and ask them in the meat department if they had chicken legs, then giggle and tell them to just wear pants and no one would notice. I am so sorry to those costumed children on Halloween who were clobbered by water balloons and had your candy bags taken from you (I *know*, terrible, right?), probably thereafter spending years in therapy well into adulthood.

And I apologize to Roess' Market for the five-finger discount of that candy bar on the other side of the far register, by the drinking fountain. Not sure what I was thinking ... clearly I wasn't. I later felt very remorseful about this—especially since the kind deli man would always give kids a free slice of bologna for the asking. Lest you think I was completely without a conscience,

I did go back one day and secretly left allowance money on the counter by a register.

The reader might be glad to know that I (mostly) grew out of these poor choices of youth, and my trail to juvenile delinquency didn't lead to a life of crime. I was lost in a wilderness of poor judgment choices and consequences, but found my way out of the dark forest, into the Light. If I did have to pay any penitence, it was that my own kids, at times, misbehaved similarly, and it grieved me to no end. But, thankfully, they too made it to responsible adulthood ... with a little fun along the way too. *Did I just write that out loud?*

Chapter Twenty
HEAD IN THE CLOUDS

"Your hopes, dreams and aspirations are legitimate. They are trying to take you airborne, above the clouds, above the storms, if you only let them." —William James

MOUNT EVANS (14,264 FT.), MOUNT EVANS WILDERNESS, COLORADO

Wow, if I could get paid for dreaming, and dreaming big, I'd be a rich man! I've got no shortage of aspirations, goals and challenges that I'd still like to take on. Sometimes it seems, however, that it's hard to fly with my feet nailed to the ground by life's circumstances, or my own limitations, real or perceived.

What if hopes and dreams are never fulfilled? What if we don't even try to accomplish some of them? What disappointments and regrets will we have later? How will that shape who we are and who we will become?

American author and humorist Mark Twain (Samuel Clemens) said something on this subject that resonated with me: "Twenty years from now you will be more disappointed by the things you didn't do than by the things you did. So throw off the bowlines. Explore. Dream. Discover."

One of my father's good friends, Jim Vaughn, a fit man in his 60s at the time, could not be accused of failing to accomplish many fine things in his life. Jim is an involved and loving husband, father and grandfather, now great-grandfather. In his career, he had helped several businesses achieve success, and he has been active many years as a lay leader in his church. One unfulfilled dream Jim had was to climb a Colorado 14,000-foot peak.

Jim had met many challenges head-on in his life, some through his years of service to his country in the U.S. Navy. But did he have the stuff to summit one of the geographically highest land points in the contiguous 48 states? He had the drive, passion and heart, but did he have the stamina, legs and lungs to make it to the top? Age plus elevation can create quite an obstacle to high-country climbing success.

Someone once said, "A goal is a dream with a deadline." Jim —if he could—was going to make this happen. And the sooner, the better. He wasn't getting any younger!

Jim accepted my offer to guide and help him up his first fourteener. Obviously, he had not heard other stories about folks I took up fourteeners, and I didn't mention them. Seriously, I was delighted to be a part of this adventure in his life. This was the fulfillment of a life goal for Jim.

I recommended we try Mount Evans, a good starter peak. Mount Evans and Mount Bierstadt (peaks connected by a saddle) have the distinction of being two of the closest fourteeners to Denver. Evans is just 36 miles west of Colorado's downtown capitol building and has a paved road to the summit—one of only two fourteeners with improved roads to the top.

In the late 1800s, Denver and Colorado Springs were in a race for the hearts, minds and dollars of eastern tourism. In 1888, the Cascade and Pikes Peak Toll Road Company completed a 16-mile graded road up the north side of Pikes Peak. In 1917, Denver's mayor procured state funds to build a road to the top of Mt. Evans. It took 10 years to complete.

The Mount Evans Scenic Byway is the highest paved road in the United States. We were not going to drive all the way to the top and count it as a climb. Tempting. But, no, we'd use our legs to summit.

I'm often asked by those wanting to climb their first fourteener, What's an easy one, to start with?"

The truth of it is that there are no easy 14ers. Of the 54 (some books list 58) mountains over 14,000 feet, there are by comparison, *easier* ones, but none easy as most might judge easy. About 10 - 12 fit into this easier category, with the rest progressively more difficult. Evans falls into that first group defined by difficulty as Class 1 or Class 2 (Classification goes up to Class 5 which is technical climbing requiring ropes.).

Jim and I intended to start a customized climb from a parking area at Summit Lake beneath Mt. Evan's north face. Jim, dressed in a striped sweatshirt, jeans, tennis shoes and a green, lumber company sports cap, stretched outside my SUV. He looked up the mountain with anticipation.

"How you feeling? Ready to try?" I asked.

Jim grabbed his small backpack and crooked wood hiking stick. "Ready to do it," he said, without a hint of hesitation in his voice.

We traveled close to the road before we began our improvised ascent up the broad Northeast Ridge. Passing the lake outlet and looking out on the alpine setting of the high cirque, we encountered a small herd of shaggy mountain goats. They were unimpressed by our presence, obviously used to gawking, camera-clicking visitors.

There is no trail up on this particular route. We could see the top, knew where we needed to go and simply began to make our way upward. The going was a little slow as we traversed over patches of tundra, shifting rock under foot and even some snow. Although not the standard trail to the top, the books still offer this path as an alternative. The remaining snowdrifts in early summer impeded our progress as each carefully placed step had to be dug into the banks. I'm sure the cold, wet snow filled Jim's tennis shoes, but he never complained. Perhaps I should have mentioned to him that hiking boots would have been a good idea.

Although this is an "easier" route up a fourteener, it is one that catches many unprepared climbers off guard. It is very exposed to bad storms and lightning. Fortunately, we had started early and continued to have good weather, but we wanted to keep a certain pace in case that changed suddenly, as happens often in the summertime.

As we crested the ridge—huffing and puffing—it was jarring to see the signs of civilization (cars on the road and the first peek at the observatory on the top) with a half mile to go to the summit. A tourist greeted us at the edge of the parking lot with "Hey, did you guys *climb* up the side of the mountain?" We smiled and nodded, breathlessly, and I bit my lip, repressing a snarky comeback.

We passed the observatory dome, the road, parking area and the remaining rock foundation and walls of the Crest House. Also known as Summit House, the restaurant/gift shop was built during the summers of 1941 and 1942 but burned in 1979 and was not rebuilt.

Another 130 vertical feet through a series of short switchbacks to the top and we made it. After a congratulatory high-five and a hug, with pride and gratitude, Jim surveyed his accomplishment. He took his time to enjoy the fulfillment of a dream. I know it was hard, a little painful and a bit beyond what he thought he could do, but he had done it.

Dr. Laura Schlessinger once said, "Self-esteem must be earned. When you dare to dream, dare to follow that dream, dare to suffer through the pain, sacrifice, self-doubts and friction from the world. You will genuinely impress yourself."

Like Jim, I hope I always keep dreaming. I hope I keep aspiring to new accomplishments well into my 60s and 70s. Why not dream, explore, discover and take flight above the clouds? I look forward to the next great adventure in my life, whatever that might be. And, whether I succeed or fail, at least I will have tried.

Chapter Twenty-One
THESE WERE REAL BUTTES

"We must go beyond textbooks, go out into the bypaths and untrodden depths of the wilder-ness and travel and explore and tell the world the glories of our journey."—John Hope Franklin

PAWNEE NATIONAL GRASSLAND, WELD COUNTY, COLORADO

THEY WERE WAY, waaay, out there. We're talking Nebraska-Kansas out there, far from my familiar Colorado Springs region. They are called the Pawnee Buttes.

I read about the buttes, and had wanted to see them for myself. From my research, I should have known how remote these predominant geologic features really were, located at the Pawnee National Grassland, and by the directions I had downloaded from websites. (I'm kinda old school that way, printing out directions, not just relying on my cell phone GPS/navigation app.)

Some warnings from web sites read, "They're a little tricky to find," "The Pawnee Buttes are literally out in the middle of nowhere, so it would be best to come prepared with a detailed map," and "Many roads in this area are dead ends and some only serve private ranches." At one point in my pre-dawn start, I saw a posted sign that read, "No gas for the next 60 miles." After following about 47 directional turns through a maze of county roads, continually resetting my odometer, I arrived at the small trailhead parking lot, glad that I had stopped for convenience-store coffee along the way, and equally happy that there was a public restroom here, and that it was open. Relieved, I started my hike.

A five-mile round trip trail system would take me to an overlook point, and then down to the base of each of the two buttes that rise 300 feet above the surrounding prairie. These windswept plains, with such a rich frontier history—punctuated by the tragedy of the Dust Bowl on the western edge of the Great Plains—was a new hiking experience for me compared to my usual Rocky Mountain adventures. This grassland, besides being known for the Pawnee Buttes, is the area where James Michener set his historic novel *Centennial*. Michener changed the name of the prominent features to the "Rattlesnake Buttes," and the fictional town of Centennial was actually a combination of the contemporary nearby towns of Sterling, Ault and Keota.

As I headed to the Overlook bluff, a gentle breeze stirred the grass along the side of the trail. Tall bunches of yellow-orange sunflowers punctuated my way. Seemingly endless vistas to the horizon did eventually kiss a blue and gray sky as rain clouds began to build from the south. I had the whole grasslands to myself; 193,060 acres of big country was mine alone to explore. And explore I did, through canyons and gullies, up hills, navigating between delicate clay hoodoos and around the bases of the buttes themselves.

At one point, to my right, I caught sight of a rather large snake warming itself in the sunshine on a flat rock. In that I've never seen a rattlesnake in all my years hiking in Colorado, I cautiously approached it. I know, dumb, I suppose, but I was curious. As I drew closer, no startling rattle noise greeted, or warned, me. The snake—unidentified by me—was not a rattler. It showed less interest in me, than I it, and slowly slithered off in search of breakfast.

A different kind of trail: The eastern plains of Colorado are beautiful too.

The two Pawnee Buttes rule over the prairie, tall as massive 20-story buildings, the West Butte looking like a grand courthouse and the East Butte like a giant bell. Each has a double cap of limestone protecting the soft sandstone of their bases. The buttes were not to be climbed as the walls were not only steep and technical, but are not rock but loose, crumbly sediment. I followed the rules and enjoyed them from below.

A rapidly darkening sky quickened my pace back to the car. Large rain drops pelted my lightweight windbreaker and splatted the soft soil of the trail. The wind moved the sunflowers like metronomes. I'm a sucker for historic windmills. I was glad I had just enough time to take some photos of windmills close to the trailhead before the heavens opened up to a deluge.

The drive home didn't go nearly as smooth as my morning travel adventure, as challenging as that was. Trying to reverse the directions, I missed this-and-that turn and found myself hopelessly lost in vast ranch land in the middle of no where, *somewhere*. Out deep in Michener's fictional Centennial-land. It's kind of exciting—an adventure, really—to not know exactly where you are, and to try to figure it out. More fun to be lost in the wilderness than, say, in a bad part of town, late at night in a big city.

Someone once said, "It feels good to be lost in the right direction." I could have stopped and asked for directions, if anyone was around. I suppose I could have used my cell phone GPS app, but that would have been too easy. The early pioneers didn't have Google Maps. I knew that if I just continued to drive west, toward the mountains, I would eventually reach the interstate and could take that south to the Springs. The problem was that I was so far out, I couldn't even see the mountains!

Obviously, I did find my way home, a bit embarrassed and tired. A long day. But glad for trail memories of something completely different.

Chapter Twenty-Two
ROLL OUT OF A PREDICAMENT

"By failing to prepare, you are preparing to fail." — Benjamin Franklin

BRAINARD LAKE, COLORADO

AHHH ... springtime in the Rockies! What a wild weather ride it is. Let's just say that spring and summer arrive late where I live. Our spring seems like a continuation of winter months most years. Fortunately, when we do get late snow, much of it melts by the next day, at least at the lower elevations. It's all so welcome, charming, romantic and sentimental around Christmas. But by the end of April, we just want to strangle Colorado weather's neck. It's not unusual to get one last spring snowstorm as late as mid-to-late May!

While we get the quicker melt where we live and can again see our greening grass, this is not so in the high country. One April I had hiked up around Brainard Lake, northwest of the city of Boulder. The lake sits at 10,525 ft. in a glacially-carved valley — quite a dramatic setting surrounded by the high mountains of the Indian Peaks Wilderness Area.

I had gone snowshoeing to this scenic setting several years prior and wanted to revisit. Wow, what a shock. The snow was so high around the still-frozen lake that in some areas the drifts were up to the bottom of the road signs. I understand that the Rocky Mountains that year got about 120 percent of the average annual snowfall. Good for our thirsty reservoirs.

Soon into my three-mile round-trip trek, I wished I had again brought my snowshoes. What was I thinking? Talk about being unprepared! As I tromped around the edge of the mostly-iced-over lake, with hiking boots and gaiters only, I post holed with every exhausting step. At one point I sank with both legs into the deep snow past my thighs. The more I struggled to get out, the more stuck I felt. I thought I might have to just stay there totem-pole-frozen until the full summer thaw. It was like being in icy quicksand, I imagined.

I rocked back and forth to little evacuation progress. With my hiking stick, I stabbed around my legs, hoping to loosen up the trap, then leaned on it to try to get at least one leg free. I thought about just what were the rules for getting out of quicksand. I laid back flat on my pack and started rolling back and forth at the waist, with the weight off my legs. I was able to get one leg free, then the other. With one last big push, I rolled out of my predicament, and down into a small gully. I was free! My effort had to be an unpleasant and ungraceful sight I'm sure, if anyone else had been around to see it.

Brainard Lake, sitting before a half-circle audience of snow-covered peaks, was as beautiful as I had remembered. As I circled the lake, I stayed away from the higher drifts. Two deer appeared out of the forest, no doubt taking advantage of the warmth of the sun on this cloudless day. They paid no attention to me. A couple of ducks searched the lake edge for any open water. I guess I should come back some summer or fall for an entirely different view of this lovely, pristine landscape. At least I wouldn't have to push through all this snow … in springtime!

Chapter Twenty-Three
HELEN'S ANGELS

"I dream of hiking into my old age."—Marlyn Doan

ALDERFER RANCH/THREE SISTERS PARK, EVERGREEN, COLORADO

I HIKE. I discover. I observe and report. Sometimes I struggle on trails or outright fail, get lost or fall down—but that can all be part of the story. I do all this because I love being in the wilderness, and I hope to inspire others to go out and do something similar (except for the failing, getting lost and falling down).

I don't go out specifically looking for stories. Sure, I do hope to find them. But they usually find and surprise me, and often in unexpected ways. Such was my hike in Alderfer Ranch/Three Sisters Park, a designated Jefferson County Open Space outside of Evergreen, Colorado.

I was interested to survey this 1,128-acre wilderness park. I had learned from my online research that this area—just about an hour and a half from my home—was a mix of hiking scenery including lush, emerald meadows, marshy bogs with croaking frogs, huge granite boulder piles, and ponderosa pine forests, all accessed through 18 miles of intersecting trails.

Soon into my exploration, I climbed a granite rock pyramid

to get an elevated perspective of the region. Looking across the open grassland, encircled by thick woods, I could see some of the original ranch buildings by the trailhead parking lot. The Alderfer family operated a sawmill, raised silver foxes and pastured horses. The original property and the surrounding land was purchased in segments by Jefferson County from 1977 to 2002. The public and I can now enjoy this beautiful park crisscrossed with well-maintained, moderate-effort trails. Not all of my hiking and climbing has to be extreme to be enjoyed. In fact, the flatter the terrain, the less chance I have of falling down.

Halfway through my hike, on a steeper portion near the base of one of the Three Sisters (three dramatic, connected rocky rises out of the forest) and a brother, I came upon a group of elderly hikers sitting trailside on boulders, resting and rehydrating. I stopped and we chatted for a while. At first I thought my story from this trip might be some history of the Alderfer Ranch or the heavy-set triplet sisters. But instead, meeting this group of seniors, passionate about hiking, was my story ... well, their story.

I discovered that their hiking group had a name: Helen's Angels (named, appropriately, by their founder, Helen Angel). Most were in their 80s, with their youngest member being 78 years old. They hiked moderate wilderness trails regularly together, although their numbers (currently about 30 of them) and their pace had dwindled a bit.

"We were not always this old," Dick said, the one gentleman with the group of ladies this day, and the oldest at 86. "Somehow, that just happened," he added with a twinkle in his eye. Dick had a toothy, contagious smile, two hiking sticks, two hearing aids, two manufactured knees, and too buoyant of an attitude for a man of his age.

Most of Helen's Angels had been hiking together for over 30 years. Back in the beginning, Helen and a couple of girlfriends were involved in leading some Girl Scouts, and one day when a trail hike was planned and no girls showed up, the ladies decide to go hiking anyway. So started years of trail adventuring together, shared memories and deepened friendships. Today, not every member can make every hike, and some weathered by the years, can hike no longer. Others, like Helen herself, now hike with the angels in heaven.

I hope that one day when my hair is white or missing altogether (along with my teeth), when my old bones and muscles are failing me, and the spring in my step is a bit more like Fall, I will still be full of life and have an enthusiasm for the wilderness like the Angels whom Helen inspired. I'd like that to be *my* story.

Some of the young-at-heart members of Helen's Angels hiking club.

Chapter Twenty-Four

FOR THE LOVE OF PANCAKES

"I'm going to have pancakes, with a side of pancakes."—Anonymous

PANCAKE ROCKS TRAIL, TELLER COUNTY, PIKES PEAK REGION, CO

I'M A SIMPLE GUY, I guess. When all of my friends are posting intense political rants or going off on social issues, I'm posting a photo of the distorted Mickey Mouse-shaped pancake I just made.

What can I say? I love pancakes. I will have to admit that I am somewhat traditional—as well as a bit boring, I suppose—about how I love to love them. Just butter and hot maple syrup on top, please, and I'll be very satisfied. No need to load them with tons of other stuff. Keep it simple. But give me loads: mounds of silver-dollar sized or tall stacks as wide as a dinner plate, I don't care. And maybe throw some bacon on the side too. Yum.

My love for pancakes might explain why I wanted to hike to Pancake Rocks. Now, I knew the natural rock formations would not be made out of *real* pancakes. Duh! (Not like my delightful trip to Big Rock Candy Mountain, where the rocks really were made of real sweets.) The concept of pancake-shaped rocks intrigued me; that's not something you see every day.

The 6.9 mile round trip Pancake Rocks Trail (with a bonus side trip to Horsethief Falls) is about an hour drive up into the mountains from Colorado Springs, midway between the small town of Divide and the historic gold mining (now gambling) community of Cripple Creek. The trailhead is a little tricky to find, as there isn't even a road sign announcing its start. The research I had done in preparation for the hike described the trail as moderate to strenuous, with an elevation gain of about 1,200 feet to a 10,932 ft. summit. I didn't find it too difficult, but then I live at 7,200 ft. and had hiked all summer.

The trail begins steeply from the small parking area next to the closed Little Ike Tunnel. It opens up into a nice valley with rolling hills and beaver ponds. From here I climbed a series of switchbacks through a dense conifer forest. Along the way, visible through the pines, are a series of flat, pancake-like rock formations. If you'd like to try this trail too, do not be fooled: Although picturesque in their own way, these are not the pancakes you are looking for. Keep moving forward to where the forest thins out and the trail clearly ends.

Imagine my delight when I reached my destination and was standing on a big stack of pancakes overlooking a dramatic valley with Cripple Creek to the south and mountain ranges in the background toward the west. The mostly solid rock outcroppings, stacked one on top of the other, had been worn away by centuries of wind and rain. They really did resemble pancakes. My stomach growled.

Now, to be fair, I must mention two things: 1) The location could probably have been called "Cow Patty Trail" by the look of the stacked, flat rock shapes that surrounded me, but that wouldn't have sounded nearly as appealing, and 2) Yes, you could see the pancake shapes (with some imagination), but they looked like the grotesque and distorted pancakes I used to make my kids on Saturday mornings when they were young.

Because I was an artist, the young'uns just assumed that my skillet could be a hot canvas, and they would shout out shape requests for animals, trains, bicycles, houses or their names in calligraphy. The best I could usually come up with was a disappointing oblong donut shape or a scary cartoon character head. Hey, pancake batter is a difficult medium to work with. I'd eat the rejects that were too burnt, those that came off the griddle in pieces, or were just too gross (no one wants to eat what looked like a jellyfish-shaped pancake). With extra butter and maple syrup, I didn't care what they looked like, just how yummy they tasted.

Chapter Twenty-Five
MEETING MOSES AND ZEUS

"This is the sense of the desert hills, that there is room enough and time enough."—Mary Hunter Austin

ALCOVE SPRING TRAIL, TAYLOR CANYON, CANYONLANDS, UTAH

I'M NOT TOO IMPRESSED by celebrities. Having grown up in Southern California, I was often exposed to sports, media and Hollywood types in public settings. When I could drive, my friends and I would go to Westwood or to Hollywood to view a movie on the "big, big screen" (like the historic Cinerama Dome theater on Sunset Boulevard, opened in 1963) and we would frequently see actors enjoying dinner out or a night at the cinema.

It seems like back in those days, paparazzi crowding in on celebrities' personal space was not such a regular occurrence. Stars could enjoy an outing just like regular folks, and I was happy to leave them alone as well. I remember taking my young children to the Magic Mountain amusement park in Valencia, and in the kiddie section seeing Meryl Streep cheering on her daughter's joy and wonder on a small, goofy circular airplane ride. I didn't rush up for an autograph—this was just a little family having a nice day out like we were.

But years later, in Canyonlands National Park, in southeast Utah, the chance of being introduced to Moses and Zeus on a trail hike sounded darn interesting. This opportunity for Kevin and me when we hiked down a thousand feet off the Island in the Sky mesa, well now, that celebrity encounter could possibly impress me! Especially since Moses was 930 feet tall. One didn't see something like that in Hollywood! If Charlton Heston as Moses had been on the Cinerama Dome's 86-foot wide screen, he wouldn't have been that big. (*The Ten Commandments* came out in 1956. The first movie to play at the Cinerama Dome was *It's a Mad, Mad, Mad, Mad World*.)

This mad, mad high desert in the Moab region is so big, so expansive, it takes a good amount of time to explore it all. And Kevin and I had put in hours, days, weeks over many years, adventuring in the red sandstone canyons and scenic geological formations of Arches and Canyonlands National Parks, including the Needles District, one of my favorite regions. Island in the Sky has several trails that drop off the cliffy edges down to a 100-mile-long four-wheel-drive trail called the White Rim Road, and we had huffed and puffed down and up most of them. One that still remained for us was the Alcove Spring Trail, down to Taylor Canyon. From here, we'd continue on to meet Moses and Zeus.

The Alcove Spring Trail is a difficult, 11.2-mile round trip that covers varied terrain, with every turn offering breathtaking scenery. Less than a half mile from the trailhead, the route dropped 800 feet steeply into a deep and wide canyon. We've hiked three of four seasons (summer is just too blazing hot) in and around Moab, and we were back in winter for this trip. The trail switchbacks would have been helpful for the descent, if not covered in snow and ice. This was made worse by our failure to bring Yaktrax, cleats stretched onto hiking boots to improve traction, to help one from slipping and falling hundreds of feet to a gruesome death. We proceeded with great caution past a massive Navajo Sandstone cliff with an enormous, amphitheater-like alcove, where there is water at the bottom and for which the trail is named.

Alcove Spring played an important role in the lives of the prehistoric peoples of Canyonlands. The Anasazi Indians who lived in the canyons made frequent trips to the Island in the Sky mesa for hunting and gathering, but water is scarce on the plateau, and most of the springs are located far below the rim. The Indians could always find water in the alcove even late in the summer. This spring was also well known to the sheep and cattle ranchers who grazed their stock in the area in the late 1800s. Kevin and I were probably on the trail blazed during the early 1900s by cattlemen in order to provide water for the livestock. We stopped to drink from our water bottles. Hiking is thirsty business, even in winter.

In a slow mile and a half, we reached the broad valley of Trail Canyon. We wound down this dry wash drainage for several miles, with steep walls surrounding us on every side, on our way to Taylor Canyon. We continually referenced our topo map and watched for directional cairns, as the trail here was not well defined. We also scanned the snow for coyote pack prints, knowing that they also came to the spring for water. The route took us close to the base of the monolithic, rocky towers of Moses and Zeus, and the smaller Aphrodite, all popular with experienced rock climbers.

Okay, so why are these huge, slender spires curiously named for a biblical patriarch, the Old Testament leader of the Israelites … and a Greek mythological god of the sky and rain, and ruler of the Olympian gods? A ranger at the Island in the Sky Visitor's Center told me that Bates Wilson, the park's first superintendent, had named them to represent strength and power. Makes some sense, I guess, looking up at the huge formations, in a bizarre way of combining biblical history and ancient folklore.

The tallest of the sandstone pinnacles is the one named Moses. Without too much stretch of the imagination, the formation does look like an old man wearing a long robe, slightly hunched over as he gazes down upon the smaller spire figure of Zeus in front of him. I'm not sure why Moses would be talking to Zeus, but his posture suggests a solemn and reverent moment, as if he were about to utter something of great importance. Or maybe they're just making dinner plans. Manna? Again?

An unlikely pairing of icons: Moses and Zeus tower over Taylor Canyon.

Kevin and I slowly made our way up the 500-foot climb to the base of the rocks, careful not to slip on patches of snow in the shade. The trail was steep, covered in tricky gravel, and meandered quite a bit to avoid the shale ledges and outcroppings. We came first to the base of Zeus, then followed a sometimes vague and confusing route, with few cairns, to a narrow bench below Moses. We'd leave the rest of the over 400-foot ascent to the top of the fractured, ruddy sandstone to the professional rock climbers. This was high enough to stop for lunch and take in the spectacular 360 degree panorama of the canyons below us. This was a live Cinerama Dome on steroids!

As much as we were enjoying the views, sitting quietly at the feet of Moses, we couldn't stay too long. We had a good distance back, and we didn't want to snow climb out of the canyon in the dark. No time for celebrity autographs. We had to be on our way.

As it turned out, the last part of the hike was in moonlight anyway. We pulled out our headlamps and flashlights and guided each other back up the cliffs through the snow and ice. Stumbling tired to the car, we were satisfied that we had put in the time and effort in some big country, and had been in the presence of greatness, the power and strength of these ancient spires. This celebrity encounter did impress me!

Chapter Twenty-Six
PILLOWS AND POPCORN

"You will find more happiness growing down than up ."—
Author Unknown

ANOTHER TIME, ANOTHER PLACE, MONTE VISTA, COLORADO

IMAGINE BEING in your pajamas (I'll just let you do that), turning down the bed, fluffing the pillow, and climbing under the covers. Envision that you had already clicked off the ceiling light and had opened wide the curtains from a large picture window. The double feature drive-in movie is about to begin, just outside your motel room.

Imagine no more! This experience can be yours in Monte Vista, Colorado, at one of America's most unique lodging concepts. The Best Western Movie Manor is part of a historic drive-in movie theatre, which means guests can watch movies on the "big screen" from the comfort of their motel room every mid-May to mid-September.

In this beautiful region of southwest Colorado, I had passed this curiosity several times on my way out to the Durango area to hike segments of the Colorado Trail, to climb fourteen thousand foot peaks, or driving to hunting camp. On my way back home one fall, having completed my last section of the Colorado Trail,

I decided to finally stop and explore this place firsthand. I was tired and wanted to be home, but this odd distraction from the highway just couldn't be passed by anymore. Standing in the parking lot, I couldn't help but be transported back in time. Warm childhood memories from decades earlier flooded over me.

I grew up going to (and loving) drive-in movies. My parents would gather up my sister and me in the back seat of our family car with pillows, homemade buttered popcorn and perhaps pajamas to change into before the movie started. Off we'd go to our favorite cinema venue in Pasadena, California. We'd begin our early evening at a drive-in burger place close to the drive-in movie location. If memory serves, the establishment was similar to early McDonald's drive-ins, and was called, of all things, Peak's Burgers.

We'd arrive at the drive-in movie complex well before dusk. This was a real adventure for us kids. This drive-in had a playground down under the huge outdoor screen structure. Not only that, but this place had a small train that would transport the kids in a large oval around the base of the screen, and to imaginary travel destinations far beyond. When it started to get dark, and about the time the dancing popcorn buckets and candy boxes and singing soft drinks came across the screen, our parents would call for us. We'd load in, get settled, and in came the metal box speaker off the post and in though the window, volume to be adjusted to everyone's liking. I remember the echo-y sound emanating from every other car's speakers, windows partially rolled down, windshields all pointed toward the screen. Our parents hoped we'd not spill our popcorn and that we'd be able to wait until the intermission between the double feature to have to go to the restroom in the snack bar at the back of the lot. Too bad more kids today will never have the experience of going to the drive-in movies.

Back at the Best Western Movie Manor, a young desk clerk greeted me warmly in the lobby and was more than happy to provide me literature about the history of the motel. She also offered a fresh-brewed cup of coffee, welcomed me take a self-guided tour of the facilities, and to take as many photos as I'd like. What I really had to do was use the restroom—at my age there are a number of needed "stops" in a seven-hour trip home, especially after morning coffee.

In 1955, George Kelloff and wife Edna purchased the site of an old airport west of downtown Monte Vista and built the Star Drive-In Theater. Business grew for several years, but George wanted a more secure, year-round financial base. He imagined a novel concept in his pajamas one night. In 1964, his dream was realized by constructing a motel that would wrap around the drive-in theater and allow guests to view movies from the privacy of their rooms. Or fall to sleep to movies, being already in bed. Their choice.

In following years, the Movie Manor grew and was continuously updated. Each room is spacious and comfortable. Movie snack vending machines are right down the hall. But you can still find your favorite dancing and singing movie treats in the iconic drive-in concessions stand and bring that back to your room. Just brush the buttered popcorn out of the bed before falling asleep.

Imagine, with the setting sun creating a yellow-red glow behind the Rockies, your movies are about to begin on two screens. When the features start rolling come dark, snack bar announcements and movie soundtrack audio are piped into the room through expected lo-fi mono speakers. Reclining, with snacks surrounding you, your drive-in motel experience commences. I know what some of you are reminiscing about your bygone dates at drive-ins. That was 30 – 40 years ago, you were a teenager, and your kids may be in the movie motel room with you.

The Movie Manor gained national recognition and has been featured on PBS Television, BBC Radio, NBC Dateline, Extra, and in publications like The New York Times, Travel & Leisure Magazine, and the Smithsonian Magazine. Maybe next time, instead of passing by at 65 miles per hour, I'll have to stop for a night of drive-in movies and snacks. Everyone should have a chance to be a kid again.

Chapter Twenty-Seven
LIGHTNING FAST

"Live every day as if it were going to be your last; for one day you're sure to be right ."—Harry Harbord Morant

MOUNT YALE (14,199 FT.), COLLEGIATE PEAKS, SAWATCH RANGE, COLORADO

My granddaughter Maren could not stop talking on the Denny Creek Trail on our way to climb Mount Yale, and I loved it. Days like this with a young person were like finding lots of extra M & M's in your trail mix. Her dad Joe and I were amazed. Often, we were lucky to get just a nod and a grunt when trying to communicate with this teenager.

On our pre-dawn drive to the trailhead, we had stopped for donuts and coffee (not really the Breakfast of Champions for mountain climbers, I admit!). As it turns out, too much caffeine makes Maren very hyper … and chatty. I was not about to complain. She was in full, non-stop conversation mode (really, a monologue) about the scenic beauty of her surroundings, her love for the outdoors, her joy and excitement of summiting her next enormous peak with us (I had summited all 54 peaks—the full list at that time—but was on my second round with Maren and Joe), her colorful hiking pants (they looked more like yoga pants to me, but what do I know of women's hiking fashion?), her plans for college, Mean Girls, her love of her new hiking boots, discussing this trail stop, or that, ones to take a good photo or her, expressions of her concerns if Joe and I would be able to keep up with her to the top (of course, we couldn't maintain her youthful, highly-caffeinated pace). I was exhausted by her exuberance (but loving it) and we had just started the hike! We also talked about where we'd be going for our accomplishment-celebration dinner. We always enjoy discussing where we'd like to have our post-climb meal. Trail snacks only take you so far.

We get an early start for our 14er mountain climbs, but made a special effort this time. The goal is to get up and off the top of these monsters by noon, trying to get down the mountain (at least down to treeline) before the predictable summer afternoon thunderstorms rolled in. But this season, the weather conditions had been quite extraordinary. Huge, pounding storms were routinely coming in fast and hard by mid-morning. As a precaution, hikers were getting started at a trailhead by midnight, hitting the summit at sunrise, and getting completely off the mountain and back to their cars by noon.

One group this season wasn't so fortunate, even with their early start. This was a cautionary tale, but sometimes even with doing everything right, nature has its own plans. And this time with tragic results.

CHIP LANE AND HIS BROTHER CRAIG SUMMITED MT. YALE before 1:00 p.m. They couldn't stay long on the top enjoying the panoramic views this mid-July day, as dark clouds began rolling in quickly. They had heard the news reports about how early and fast violent storms were hitting the high country this season. They had read about the 16 hikers and a dog that had all been hit mid-morning by lightning 500 feet below Mt. Bierstadt two weeks earlier (all survived, except for the dog, Rambo, who took the brunt of the strike). Chip and Craig were determined not to become another news story this non-typical year. Thunder claps shook the ground around them in the bowl below the peak they had departed. They doubled their pace, careful not to slip on the gravel down the steep trail. They needed to get to the trees, and fast.

I had enjoyed getting to know this young man that spring and into early summer. Chip and I both worked for the Broadmoor Hotel—he, a ranch hand at Emerald Valley Ranch; me, a Wilderness Driver to the hotel's glamping resorts—and we both enjoyed high country adventuring and climbing Colorado's 14ers. I would drive Chip to the camp and we would share stories about our previous founteener conquests, as well as compare notes in preparation for upcoming hikes. We knew that we'd both be trying for a summit of Mt. Yale that season.

I had forgotten that Chip was going to climb Yale the previous week as I dove him and other staff to camp for their pre-dawn start to ready the lodge and facilities for guests. When we arrived, as everyone was disembarking the van, Chip pulled me aside.

"Hey, did you see me on the news?" he asked in a subdued voice in the dark.

"No," I said surprised, imagining that perhaps it had something to do with the hotel. "What happened?"

"We were hit by lightning on Yale," Chip said, his voice not much more than a whisper, still, understandably, shaken. "Last Friday. My brother and I were interviewed by a couple of TV stations and the story was in Denver and Colorado Springs newspapers. Four of us were hit—a direct strike—one didn't make it."

I was stunned. How did I not hear about this? I had been closely following the weather conditions on the mountains, especially with our climb scheduled for Friday of that week. I asked him what had happened.

Chip said he and Craig had done everything right, checking the forecasts, and getting their early start. They then had to get down off the top quickly as clouds were building rapidly. "We looked across the valley and saw that a storm was coming, but it still looked far away," Chip said. They started jogging down the gravely trail. A couple of other hikers followed close behind.

At the summit, they met for the first time newly-weds from Denver, Ryan Pocius and Kathleen "Katie" Bartlett. The two were on their last day of their honeymoon—a weeklong trip through the outdoors in the Rocky Mountains that was ending with a mountain climb. Both had a common passion for nature and wilderness exploration. They wanted to climb a 14er together to begin their life's journey as a married couple.

The sky turned black overhead. Katie and Ryan were literally running down, so Chip and Craig courteously stepped just off the trail. They were very nearly to the timberline.

"The last things I remember were letting them pass, and looking down at my watch that read 1:07 p.m."

Chip's recounting of the story slowed.

"When I awoke, I was 10 feet off the trail on the alpine grass. I didn't know how I got there, not remembering tripping or falling. I looked around and saw three bodies ... on the ground," he said, unable to disguise a small tremble in his voice.

He struggled to his feet and tried to make sense of the scene through a clouded mind. His head and right leg were throbbing. No one else moved. In his fog, he couldn't understand why Katie lay still there, "her clothes and shoes pretty much off her, burnt and what not."

Chip, who was an Eagle Scout, knew CPR, and had been trained by raft guiding companies as a wilderness first aid responder, limped into rescue mode. He was able to wake his brother, also a former Eagle Scout.

"What happened?" Craig asked dazedly. His ankle was the size of a grapefruit.

"I think we were all hit by lightning!" Chip returned. "And she took the direct hit."

"What now? Craig asked.

"I think she's dead," Chip choked out. "Maybe we can wake her husband."

Ryan did wake up—with a huge bump on his head— and immediately asked if we were alright!

"Yes," I replied, "but she's not."

They all stumbled over and gave their attention to Katie, who was lying face down further down the hill. They turned her over and gently moved her off the trail. Taking turns, they administered CPR. Craig then limped down the trail to flag any other hikers. As it happened, four off-duty paramedics, who were also on the mountain that day, came upon the scene and jumped in for an hour to try to save Katie's life, but they were unable to revive her.

Two of the paramedics ran down the trail to their vehicle and drove two miles to find a cellphone signal to call 911 and Search and Rescue. It took several hours for emergency crews to reach their location, where Katie, age 31, a beloved teacher of 3- to 5-year-olds at an early learning center, was pounced dead on the mountain. The Chaffee Country Coroner's Office said it appears she had died instantly.

Chip paused in his painful retelling of this horrible experience, then continued, "For Craig and I, that was the longest hike out of the forest we had ever done."

Dawn broke over the camp, a soft light growing first from the south-east end of the valley. I just couldn't believe what I was hearing. Chip could have just as easily *not* been here sharing his story by the horse stables, where I drop staff off each morning.

After a few moments, Chip continued. Ryan had suffered injuries at the scene and was flown via Flight for Life to Colorado Springs, but eventually recovered. Both Chip and Craig, amazingly, had just minor injuries and were able to walk to safety, both of them with a bit of a limp.

The brothers visited Ryan in the hospital. A clear bond can develop through shared tragedy, and survival. Chip and Craig expressed their sympathy and support. Ryan voiced his gratitude to "a wonderful group of fellow hikers and kindred spirits" who worked so hard to try to bring his Katie back.

"I was blessed," Ryan said, "to get to spend Katie's final moments with her, as her new friends gave her chest compressions, and I gave her my own life-breath … but to no avail." Chip and Craig could hardly contain their emotions.

Ryan posted this on his wife's Facebook page: "We were sharing a personal goal that we wanted to accomplish to set our marriage off right—peaking a 14er together, and we achieved that with pictures to prove it. She had said on the hike up that it was the most beautiful hike she had ever been on. She was so happy that day and she was surrounded in a bed of wildflowers as far as her eyes could see as she passed from this world to the next."

I've been able to chat with Chip other times around the hotel about his experiences that day on the mountain. He didn't go back up to work seasonally at the camp the next year, but stayed with the hotel in Guest Services. It was months until he was able to venture up into the mountains again.

"It's just heartbreaking," Chip said. "I think about it all the time still, about what happened up there—it's a life event we're never going to forget. It's just really sad that had to happen to those two. Our hearts and our prayers keep going out to Ryan, and to both his and Katie's families."

Chip is fully recovered, physically. For weeks, his arm and leg didn't seem to work just right. A this time he was a Bellman at the hotel—and a very good one. But, when the typical afternoon storms come in over the Pikes Peak Region, with even distant thunderclaps and lightning, Chip still feels a twinge of anxiety and that he needs to duck for cover.

BACK ON OUR HIKE, CHATTY MAREN HAD SLOWED DOWN, conversationally, but not in speed of ascent. There's just not enough oxygen up in the high country to keep talking all the time. Even for women hikers, although I've seen some try all the way up and down.

After climbing the steep, rocky trail through a dense forest, our path often paralleling or crossing a clear stream with bright-green mossy banks (perfect photo ops for Maren to display her new colorful hiking pants), we broke through treeline. Standing at about 12,500 feet in elevation, I was acutely aware that we were just about at the location where Chip and the others were struck by the lightning bolt. This was a sobering thought, as I looked all around at the sky for any evidence warning of bad weather. The peak summit was in view in a bright, cloudless sky.

With her youth, energy and enthusiasm, and the caffeine still running through her veins, Maren continued to outdistance Joe and me, but kept us within sight, on our way up towards the top.

She would get several hundred yards ahead of us, but then sit enjoying the views until we arrived, and then take off again. Oh, to be young again. The higher she got, however, the more she looked for some spot to hide protected in the cleft of some large rock, as a cold wind was really picking up.

Joe and I had climbed Yale several years ago, with my son, Cary, via a different route, but I didn't remember it being quite this beautiful. We advanced up into a giant bowl below the peak that was carpeted with acres of wildflowers.

Few other hikers were on the trail this day, and those who were there had gotten an earlier start, so we met them on their way down. When we reached the summit, we had the pinnacle all to ourselves. The effort is always worth the reward—what views from the top! However, our sightseeing and trail snack munching was short-lived.

At unbelievable speed, angry clouds began to encircle us, seeming to have come out of nowhere, and closed in on us with ill intent. Very exposed up high, we needed to get down to treeline quickly. We started our descent, carefully negotiating the scree and talus, connecting the dots of the cairns through the rock fields where no clear trail was evident. Within minutes, the clouds crept low into the bowl like fog wraiths. And behind them, in the dark approaching banks, huge thunderclaps.

We were running now, well aware that one slip on the gravel trail could ruin our day as much as malevolent weather. I played the scene of Chip and the others over and over in my mind, on this same mountain, in these same conditions. We now saw flashes of light in the opaque blanket that settled in over us, with ear-deafening booms immediately following.

I yelled to Maren ahead of me and to Joe who followed behind that we should spread out a few dozen yards on the trail. I knew the procedure in such a situation, and was reminded of this when Chip had told me he thought the lightning bolt that got them had hit Katie first, then jumped from her to each of the others. I wanted to make sure that if one of us was hit, the others would be okay and able to help. It started to rain, but we didn't want to stop long enough to put on our rain ponchos. We could do that when in the forest. It's not that trees don't get hit by lightning, they do, but at least there's feeling of protection getting down lower and into the woods. At least the trees were taller than us.

Even though we were hustling, it still felt like slow motion. I visualized worst-case scenarios, and what my response would be. I had taken the American Red Cross, Wilderness First Responder Class, and had attended a refresher CPR class required by the hotel, but I did not want to have to put what I learned into practice. Not that day.

The edge of the forest grew closer and closer, starting with a thin punctuation of sad-looking, scraggly, wind-twisted pines. The climate is indeed brutal in the high country. Inside the thicker, taller trees, Maren, Joe and I stopped to put on our rain gear, helping each other get covered up. A quick hydration break and we were on way again. We had made it down off the top, but were not out of the "woods" yet. It was raining heavier now, and the downpour was starting to turn the trail into slick mud and small rivulets. We'd still have to be careful for the final several miles to the parking area.

Our day didn't end like it did for Chip's group that tragic day. But it could have. None of us know how much time we have on this earth. Mary Manin Morrissey wrote, "Every day you are alive is a special occasion. Every minute, every breath is a gift from God." I accept, with gratitude each new morning, because, lightning-fast, one day, it might be my last.

Chapter Twenty-Eight

ON EMERALD POND

"They're funny things, accidents. You never have them till you're having them."—A. A. Milne

MONUMENT VALLEY PARK, COLORADO SPRINGS, COLORADO

ONE MID-JULY DAY, I took my good friend with me for an exploration of Monument Valley Park. Lance The Wonder Dog loves to get outside for adventures as much as I do. Sir Lancelot is a 12-year-old cockapoo, whose step has slowed a bit, but don't tell him that. We've hiked many miles together, and he's been a great trail companion.

This park was built by General William Jackson Palmer, an American soldier, civil engineer, industrialist, and philanthropist. General Palmer moved west after the Civil War and founded the city of Colorado Springs. After a few decades of growth, and seeing the relative unattractiveness of the city compared to the majesty of the near Rockies—the city really is an extension west of the high prairie up to the base of the mountains—Palmer determined to beautify the downtown area for both residents and tourists. He designed and built two miles of park on both sides of the creek that included planted trees, pathways, landscaping, gardens, stone walls and structures.

I had been to this wonderful city park many warm summer evenings over the years to play co-ed softball with my wife through a YMCA league. The field is well maintained, in a beautiful setting, if not a little out of the way to get to. I have many memories of team wins and losses at this park, and even running back to the car on occasions when an explosive thunderstorm interrupted the game.

I sat on a vintage stone wall and gazed dreamily at the field, remembering the many nights a teammate batted a ball deep into the center field and I ran like the wind from first base, past second and then third, and slid headfirst into home base for a game-winning "Safe!" call by the umpire. I was transported back in time to the brightly lit field and the crowds on their feet cheering me as the team put me on their shoulders, marching me back to the dugout. Okay, that is a false memory. That never happened. Sorry.

Despite the many visits to the ball field, I had never walked the length of the path on both sides above Monument Creek. It's really quite beautiful, and I suspect so any time of the year. I should have done this a long time ago.

There are benefits to having the companionship of a dog while exploring the outdoors (if the location allows), but also downsides, as I was soon to discover. Lance and I started out on the South Monument Valley Trail at the historic Van Briggle Pottery factory. This 1908 showcase building (reminiscent of Flemish farmhouses and it was placed on the National Register of Historic Places) is now owned by Colorado College, purchased and restored in 1970, and is used as the college's Facilities Services Department. We stood for a moment and overlooked Monument Creek. The origin of this prominent waterway through the Springs starts all the way at the north end of El Paso County, from the base of the reservoirs in the Front Range foothills above Palmer Lake. The creek was flowing heavy this spring following the melt off of late season snow.

Our first stop to enjoy Monument Valley Park was at a lovely pond surrounded by willow trees, the longer branches swaying slightly in a gentle breeze, tickling the top of the water. The pond —I presume cloudy-green from algae—was populated by a few ducks, dozens of geese and goslings, and a stoic heron. The flotilla of water fowl enthusiastically paddled our way, no doubt motivated by previous breadcrumb feedings by other visitors.

I had to hold Lance back as he pulled hard on his leash. Funny, he hates water, especially bath time, but he hates birds more, frequently chasing them out of our backyard. He came up just short of going headlong into the drink, perhaps having second thoughts about a swim. Also, the geese were about his same size, and loud.

We walked around the pond and I took several photos as the glistening light on the water kept changing. The geese followed us with persistence, probably in disbelief that I hadn't tossed a little snack their direction. We stopped on the other side of the pond.

An angry group of hungry-looking, angst-ridded teenage goslings splashed feverishly our direction. Not a group to mess with. Now I wished I had brought bread crumbs, corn kernels ... or pizza, gummy bears and soda for the teens. I love capturing special moments, and I wasn't going to miss this scenic opportunity, the birds now silhouetted on the water against the bright mid-morning sun.

I got down low on rocks on the shore, ready to snap the troublemakers as they drew ever closer. I was able to get a couple of shots with my cell phone camera as they approached, but I wanted to get more of a water-level view, so I crouched lower. It was about at this point that Lance decided to go into attack mode (well, as attack-y as a cockapoo can get), with foes more his size. He yanked on the leash but I was able to hold my balance on the wobbly rocks. Somehow, however, my cell phone fell out of my hand and went *plop* into the murky green shallows and disappeared below. I should have had a leash on my phone.

I knew I had just precious seconds to recover the sunken phone if I had any hopes of it being saved. On all fours, I tried to feel around where I thought it plunged, but I didn't hit the hidden bottom—the pond was deeper here than I imagined. I rolled up my sleeve and went back in again. I just prayed that the algae wasn't some kind of flesh- eating bacteria, or that I wouldn't accidentally pull up some Creature from the Green Lagoon.

It was at this time—when the water was up above my elbow, as I felt around the slimy pond floor—that a group of summer school children came upon the pond with a park guide. He was pointing out the various water fowl and I'm sure tried to screen the kids from the pond-side butt sticking up in the air, and a submerged arm in the pea soup. No doubt, he had just told them not to feed the birds … and not to play in the water.

Got it!

I expected the phone to come up with globs of emerald sludge hanging off it, but it was only slightly sickly looking. I removed the non-waterproof cover, shook it off, and wiped the phone down. No taping on the screen changed a frozen image on the screen: an out-of-focus finger with a green background. I must have accidentally hit the shutter button with my thumb as I tried in vain to catch the phone as it left my hand.

I sat the phone in the sun on an old stone wall built in the General Palmer days and hoped for the best. Lance looked at me sheepishly as I jotted notes about my visit to Monument Valley Park. I scratched him behind his ears. What are you gonna do? Slime happens. I was due for a phone upgrade anyway.

Chapter Twenty-Nine
THE MORE, THE MERRIER!

"Life is meant for good friends and great adventures."—Anonymous

SEDONA, SONORA DESERT, ARIZONA

I LOVE to get outdoors by myself, but I equally enjoy spending time adventuring in the wilderness with friends or family, whether trekking a serpentine, wooded trail through rolling foothills, hiking canyons or dry washes in the desert, or summiting a challenging mountain peak. It's fun to make discoveries together and to see how others are reacting to the beautiful scenic landscapes. Not only do we have conversation about what we are seeing, but we also then have the shared experiences to reminisce about for years to come.

I've been out to south-east Utah countless times, to the Moab region for exploring, both alone and with others. I love Canyonlands, Arches National Park, and the Needles District. I enjoy the *wildness* of the vacant high desert, there with the otherworldly red sandstone cliffs, monolithic spires and arches. This is one reason that I'd always wanted to visit Sedona, Arizona. It seemed similar to the Utah high desert to me.

I love my Rocky Mountains, but there is something special

about the desert. The desert is quite a different experience, one that I equally appreciate. There is such an aloneness (which I don't mind), an emptiness (often full of hidden life) and exceptional beauty and surprises that are hard to describe. T. E. Lawrence is quoted as saying, "This creed of the desert seemed inexpressible in words, and indeed in thought." This describes Moab perfectly for me.

I've always had Sedona, Arizona, on my bucket list for places to visit. From the photos I'd seen, Sedona reminded me much of my beloved Moab. With its high desert locale, red cliffs, eroded plateaus, curious spires, deep canyons, dry washes, scraggly pinion pines, and vast, dry, open spaces, Sedona could be the geological sister to Moab, and perhaps it is, separated by 352 miles. I had to go there one day.

You can imagine my surprise when my kids gave Diane and me a vacation gift for our 40th wedding anniversary to … wait for it … yup, Sedona! Now when I say I was surprised—and we were genuinely surprised—I should tell you that my oldest, Sarah, had been asking questions for months like, "What's a place you've never been to, but always wanted to go? And, within a day's drive from our home?" I should have recognized all the signs of clandestine planning for a milestone event celebration, but I'm a little distracted at times, missing obvious clues. Head in the clouds? Or mind lost, wandering the forest?

Anyway, our four kids (two having spouses) had saved all year to give us this wonderful gift. They were sending the two of us off for a several-day getaway … and they were all coming along! It would be an anniversary celebration, and a family vacation. And that was perfectly fine with Diane and me. The more the merrier, I say! Especially if it means time away spent with family.

Most of us packed into a Toyota van and started our drive from Colorado Springs early one summer morning. Yes, I did say summer. Probably not the ideal time to play in the sun in the desert. Sarah told us it was actually a good time to visit, especially for a group of our size, to save on the costs of a trip like this. Apparently, with temps averaging close to 100 degrees every day in the summer, this is not high season for Sedona. We could spend a lot of time in the pool. She also brought a couple of cases of bottled water. That was good. In anticipation of the desert climate, I was already terribly thirsty by the time we had only driven an hour.

Our group of road warriors included wife Diane, Sarah, her husband Joe, our granddaughter Maren, and two of my sons, Daniel and Spencer. It was great to have our youngest, Spencer, with us, this being his last family trip for awhile, as a year later he moved to Florida for new adventures of his own. Sharing the driving for the 12-hour journey to our destination made it easier on everyone. Someone taking off their shoes exposing stinky socks did not.

My oldest son Cary, his wife Adrienne and our 2-year old grandson Duren flew from Denver to Phoenix and drove to Sedona to meet up with us. Much better for the little fella than that long drive.

Sedona is located in in the Upper Sonoran Desert in northern Arizona at an elevation of 4,500 feet. When we dropped downed out of the forest drive from Flagstaff, our first views of Sedona did not disappoint. Truly, the famous red rocks and strange sandstone formations of Sedona have to be one of the most beautiful natural sights in the U. S., rivaling anything in Moab. Sedona's dramatic canyon walls present nine layers of stone from different geological periods. Landmark rock formations and buttes include Snoopy Rock (the canine from the comic strip, sleeping on top of his doghouse), Coffeepot Rock, Bell Rock, Cathedral Rock, Courthouse Butte, the Mittens, the Cow Pies and Rabbit Ears. We outdoor adventurers had our work cut out for us. So much to explore, so little time!

We coasted into Sedona on gas fumes, because *someone* (no need to mention names, an honest mistake) wasn't paying attention to the gas gauge when we blew by the last gas station for miles, too excited to stop. We were amazed when we first entered Old Town, Main Street, Sedona. This is a charming, quaint little south-western town full of shops, open-air cafes, flowers, fountains, sculptures, restaurants and quite a number of art galleries. We'd be back to this fun town a couple of times during our stay.

What a great time we all had for our family time in Sedona,

and the surrounding region! We hiked and explored. We slid down slick rocks at a stream—making fools of ourselves—at Slide Rock State Park. We grilled dinners on the patio at the rented condo. We played games, shopped, visited galleries, took a helicopter ride over and around red rock canyons, and we swam (a lot) in any one of three pools at the resort complex. Little Grandson Duren had his first beer. One photo taken of the toddler at dinner showed an empty Corona bottle (from the person next to him). It just looked like he had gone bottoms up, lime and all, with the popular Mexican Ale. Okay, it's just a joke, Child Protective Services.

And we laughed. A lot.

The whole gang went on the Courthouse Butte Loop Trail hike, which included Bell Rock. Sure enough, the formations looked remarkably like their names. It may have been one of the longest trail hikes Cary and Adrienne had taken Duren on, ridding on Cary's back. It certainly had to have been the hottest. Ridiculously hot. Like surface of the sun hot. Glad we brought all those bottles of water. The very white part of the Jones family (yes, me) were just like sizzling bacon out there.

Daniel, our stand-up-comic son (yes, for real), the former Marine, thought he would make a series of funny videos in the desert. You know, like the hilarity of dying of thirst, and having your bones picked clean by vultures. Those types of funny short films one might find on YouTube. He'd put these on his promotional Facebook site to start with. Leaving the main Courthouse trail (Diane and Sarah chose to slow-bake under minimal shade of a scraggly tree-bush), several of us climbed about halfway up Bell Rock, in its own way a butte-like formation, overlooking the Courthouse Butte. We rested and sizzled some more.

Daniel went off a few yards to video record a skit he had prepared. Not so far away from us that we couldn't hear his monolog, he filmed himself saying things like, "Here I am in the middle of nowhere … in the desert … all by myself … with no water … I don't think I can last much longer …."

It was about at this time that he began to be pelted with small pebbles. Both Joe and Maren were trying so hard not to laugh as they showered him with gravel.

"What are you doing?" he complained loudly. "I'm trying to work over here!"

Instead of just going with it, he got upset that his little comedic skit was interrupted. That just made Joe and Maren, and the rest of us, for that matter, laugh all the harder! And fling more pebbles at him. Daniel agreed with me later that had he just continued filming, and even scanned over to someone throwing rocks at him—as he was "all alone and dying in the desert"—that might have been even funnier.

One afternoon—on our last full day there—while the ladies and little Duren splashed again in one of the pools at the resort, the men went out to get in one more hike. I had wanted to see Red Rock State Park. I had read that it was an overlooked hidden gem of red sandstone rock, piñon and juniper woodlands, and with Oak Creek flowing through the middle of the park. The lush greenery of the creek banks are an oasis in the high desert. We did a the 5-mile network of interconnecting loop trails.

At one point on a trail, we all began to smell a terrible odor. It was a stench I had smelled before but couldn't identify. We let our noses lead off-trail to a partially decomposed deer carcass. We could not see how it met its demise. But, boy, did it stink!

Our comic Daniel could not miss this opportunity for another skit. He pulled out his cell phone.

"How you doin' fella?" he asked as he filmed the still buck. "You alright?"

Daniel poked the deer with a stick, because, of course, that's what boys—even grown boys—do with dead things. He panned the rest of us watching in a combination of horror and hilarity.

"Leave it alone," older brother Cary scolded.

Daniel kept filming. "No, I think he's going to be okay. You okay, boy? Try to get up. You can do it!" Daniel nudged it with his hiking boot.

Appalled—no, more like mortified at this point, especially with other hikers coming down the trail towards us—Cary yelled, "Stop it ... stop kicking it!"

"I'm not kicking it. I'm nudging it. Nudging!" Daniel said. "Come on, fella! You *can* do it! Get up!"

Brothers. Cary was red faced. This just spurred Daniel on. The others of us were trying hard to stifle our amusement. Soon, unable to contain it any longer, we all burst out in laughter ... even Cary. I thought I even saw just a hint of a smile on the deer's face too.

We all had a great family time in Sodona, even with the sizzling-hot temp, and the rock throwing and the deer poking. I enjoy the solitary experience in the wilderness. But I would not have taken these special family memories back with me had I just gone out hiking by myself.

Family adventures, memories for a lifetime: Dad and his boys (l to r) Spencer, Cary, Daniel.

Chapter Thirty

CURSES, DEFOLIATED AGAIN!

"Bee to the blossom, moth to the flame; Each to his passion; what's in a name?"—Helen Hunt Jackson

MT. MUSCOCO, NORTH CHEYENNE CANYON, PIKE NATIONAL FOREST

OFFICIALLY, they are named Douglas-Fir Tussock Moths and Western Spruce Budworms. I just call them Tiny Agents of Darkness. I guess they are just doing what moths and worms do, but what havoc they've done. Larva from these two types of moths just happen to eat the needles from conifer trees. As a result, they have turned brown nearly 5,000 acres of forest around Cheyenne Mountain above Colorado Springs. I wish the little buggers had just flown into flames. It should be noted that this forest chomping is a different problem than the devastation caused by the pine beetle in so many parts in the state.

I had been assigned a freelance article for *The Springs* magazine to hike the foothills above Colorado Springs to see first hand how bad the tree damage was in North Cheyenne Canyon, especially on the Mt. Muscoco Trail. This moderate hike shares the first half mile with the Mt. Cutler Trail before veering off to a west ridge to Muscoco. There is wide-spread evidence on this north side of the canyon of moth damage, with a good portion of the trees stripped of needles, a few branches still showing tuffs of life. Yet, as with a forest fire, some intermittent conifers were untouched, and the ponderosa pines seemed to have escaped altogether.

At the well-marked trail split, I met Larry, a Vietnam veteran visiting from Ft. Worth, and trying to get in as many Pikes Peak Region experiences as he could in four days. In our brief conversation—he with a thick, but charming Texas drawl—we discovered that we were both wilderness trail writers, with his developing craft taking the course of inspirational nature poems.

We said our goodbyes and I continued onward and upward on a ridge, in awe of dramatic views of large rock outcroppings, the canyons below, and the panorama of Colorado Springs which blended into prairieland east, all the way to the Kansas border.

The higher I ascended, the less tree damage I saw. Looking across to Cheyenne Mountain, I could see none of the browned forest from my vantage point. Seems that the severity was not so wide spread, but regionalized. Good news. And I later read that the affected trees may not be as dead as their appearance suggests. The needles are gone, but the trees may live on. We'd have to see the next spring when the spraying of these trees was scheduled to start.

The trail climbed steeply and became more difficult with nasty roots and slippery gravel areas. At the summit, giant, lichen-covered boulders gave me a still welcome. Late afternoon light cast a yellow glow and elongated rock and tree shadows. The chimes from the Will Rogers Shrine of the Sun Tower above the Cheyenne Mountain Zoo, carried on a gentle breeze, met the rushing sound of Helen Hunt Falls below (named for the playwright, not the actress). Larry would have appreciated the poetry of the moment.

Chapter Thirty-One
SUCCEEDING AT FAILURE

"I like failure because it's so easy to achieve." —Anonymous

WILDERNESS, WANDERING, UNCOMPAHGRE NATIONAL FOREST, COLORADO

My Final Bow, Maybe

I SAT LOOKING out my home office window at freezing fog doing its frosty magic on the pine tree boughs. Three inches of fresh snow covered the yard from the night before. It was completely quiet as the workforce was sluggish to head out on icy roads, with low visibility. And the local school district had delayed students' arrival by two hours.

Seems that this midwinter we were seeing snowstorms about every two days or so. I barely got the snow shoveled off the porch and driveway when, here came another dump. The joy of the holiday season was behind us. The snow in Colorado, when it first arrives in late fall, is so charming, so beautiful, so serene, announcing the sentimentality of the days to come. By April, and even as late as May, we are shaking an angry fist at the sky. We've had it! So, stuck indoors, instead of dreaming of the White

Christmas that had passed, I reflected back on being outdoors during the last hunting season.

I hadn't been archery hunting for years. Frankly, the abysmal lack of success a decade and a half earlier had left me seriously unmotivated to hike miles in the dark, through dense forests—with no trails, and seemingly uphill in both directions—to try to get within 20 yards of game, just to play Indian with a bow and arrow. And this is assuming that you even *see* any deer or elk that have every unfair advantage on you in the wilderness. With my failure rate, if I had been born in another time and place, say as a Native American, my tribal name would have been "Hunts Like a Blind Man."

Yet, here I was again, deliberately punishing myself, this time with my son-in-law, Joe. Although Joe had a lot of experience and success back in his home state of Georgia, this would be his first opportunity to fail with me at bow hunting in the Rocky Mountains. Joe had wanted me to go with him for his first Colorado hunting time, so I reluctantly agreed. Perhaps the weight of *shared* disappointment wouldn't be so crushing.

Our elk tent camp at Owl Creek Pass in the Uncompahgre National Forest in southwest Colorado sat in an open meadow surrounded by craggy, forbidding mountain peaks, with thick forests at their feet. Joe, our good friend Bill and I dressed each morning before dawn in our camo clothing (this year wearing knit masks instead of face paint for disguise, and deciding *not* to spray ourselves in elk urine). We headed out with delusional anticipation of success from either working hard, being smart or getting lucky.

Our spirits were high. You see, with hunting there is always the possibility, the *hope*. Each day might be *the* day to "bag" something, thus creating campfire stories to recount in exaggerated detail for years to come. At least that's what we'd tell ourselves.

One evening, Joe and I decided that the next day we'd spend all day out (not returning to camp for lunch and a siesta), plus we'd spend the night out in the woods as well. That way, we'd already be set up for the next morning in the deep forest in a good location, having hiked many miles and several hours from camp. This was a first for me—and the last time I'll even think of doing such a hare-brained thing. Good idea, perhaps; poor execution.

With past hunts, I'd return to camp at the end of a long day, sometimes well after dark. Dead tired, my hunting buddy and I would crash into our respective cots after a hurried, but hot, camp dinner of Dinty Moore beef stew. At least we enjoyed the relative security and protection of our camp and large tent. This time, the notion of sleeping out in the dark woods, with hidden eyes watching us, seemed like a grand—but intimidating—adventure. Bill wisely chose to stay in the valley.

We got up into high elevation that day—nearly to tree line. It was a long and hard climb, steep and rocky, and it was compounded by the fact that we did not have the right equipment for our undertaking. We didn't have frame backpacks to carry all our overnight stuff, just lightweight daypacks. We had used bungee cords to strap on our two-man tent, sleeping bags, ground pads, heavier jackets, game field-dressing supplies, camp lights and extra food.

We *looked* ridiculous: Bulky plastic trash bags shot out in every direction. And it *felt* even worse! Our small packs were never meant to handle the added bulk. Items kept shifting and bouncing. Our shoulders and hips hurt, and our balance was thrown off as our supplies flopped around, hit tree branches and triggered ergonomic stress.

Most of the day was spent, painfully, just going to where we were going, without much hunting. With our loud shambling around in the forest, any game that day were probably several ridges, or miles, away … and laughing. Close to dusk, we decided to call it a day. Neither Joe nor I fully realized just how steep the surrounding forest floor was where we found ourselves. There was nowhere flat to pitch our tent. We scouted until dark and finally found a small, *somewhat* level spot—at least it looked nearly flat, in the dark, and in our exhausted minds.

Headlamps on, looking around for any glowing eyes in the murk, we tossed up the tent. Joe asked if we should use the tent stakes, and I assured him that our weight would hold the tent down without them. We had a snack dinner inside our cramped tent, climbed into our sleeping bags ... and then realized we were on far more of a slope than we had thought. Immediately, we—in our bags, on our pads, with our packs, and all of our extra stuff—began to slide forward toward the tent entrance. Too tired to make any adjustments, we both just kept pushing ourselves up through the rest of the long, and mostly sleepless, night.

I must have finally dozed off a bit, because just after dawn I awoke and found myself in the bottom of my sleeping bag, curled in a fetal position, knees against the zippered entrance to the tent. All our supplies were crammed in around us. Grumbling, Joe and I got dressed, stuffed our mummy bags, set them outside the tent and stumbled stiffly into the chilly first morning light. After shaking off the cramps, blinking and rubbing our eyes, we made a discovery: We hadn't just slipped down inside the tent, but the whole now-wonky tent itself had crawled, with us in it, about 10 yards down the mountainside. We were amazed and chuckled at the absurdity of it all.

At this point—maybe getting back at me for the poor advice about the tent stakes—Joe thought it would be funny to give my tightly bound sleeping bag a kick, moving it down the hill. We were both stunned to see it pick up speed, hit and bounce off rocks and logs and just ... keep ... rolling. It seemed that it wasn't going to stop, becoming its own perpetual motion bag of down feathers. When it finally slowed to a stop just a few feet from a 200-ft drop-off, Joe was bent over double in laughter. He sobered when I told him he had to go retrieve the bag, now about 50 yards away.

Given the lack of sleep, and the thought of the arduous climb back out with the ridiculous load on our backs, we decided not to hunt that morning but instead just head back to base camp. The way down was somewhat easier, but we still had the metronome walk from all the shifting weight. Bill cheerfully greeted us at camp with an "I told you so" grin on his face. After a small but convenient brunch of beef jerky and a Snickers bar, I pulled my cot out of the tent and napped in the shade of a large pine tree. A gentle breeze in no way hinted of the bad weather to come.

Late in the afternoon, rested and undeterred by our recent hunting debacle, we all dressed up like the forest again, grabbed our bows (and not much more!) and headed out. The three of us split up to cover an area surrounding a formation called Chimney Rock. I saw no game, or even signs that game had been there in a decade. I needed to find cover quickly if there was even a snowman's chance of something walking by me at dusk.

I rounded a turn on an old game trail into thick deadfall and was surprised to see a grouse sitting on a log in the open. The large bird (a bit smaller than a pheasant) must have heard me coming and stood statue-still, thinking its tan tones would camouflage it. I did have a small game permit, so I thought I'd give the 10-yard shot a try. This would be a first for me.

Carefully, I notched an arrow, lifted the bow up, pulled the bowstring back to full draw, adjusted lower than my top sight pin, held my breath and let the arrow fly. Success! I hit low on the target, but we'd still have fresh game for dinner that night. I never did find my arrow, buried somewhere deep in the brush dozens of yards away. In traditional Indian fashion, I thanked the wild bird for giving its life for me so that we'd have something other than gorp (trail mix: Good 'Ol Raisins and Peanuts) to eat that evening.

Of course, the guys were surprised back at camp when I proudly displayed my kill. It wasn't the elk we'd come for, but we would have fun sharing it for dinner, with some other meal items we could muster up. As I "dressed" it outside of our large outfitters tent, the light rain that had started on our way back grew heavier. We secured things around the tent and dashed inside.

My culinary skills are limited to begin with, but it didn't help that for our game bird entrée we had no spices, not even salt and pepper. Digging through my food box I found a small packaged container of pineapple, with juice—perfect! If you could go to a Chinese restaurant and order orange chicken, then why couldn't we have pineapple grouse? Everyone admitted it was delicious …

and, wait for it ... agreed that it tasted like ... chicken. We crashed into our cots to the sustained, soothing tippy-tap of rain on the tent.

It rained all through the night, and into the next morning—our day to pack up and return home. After three days in the wilderness, we all could stand a little "freshening up." Besides, we all wanted to be clean and dressed in something other than camo for the six-hour drive home. And so our wives would appreciate that homecoming hug.

Someone suggested (okay, it was me) that we just shower outside in the rainstorm. The temp had dropped considerably, and the rain was now coming down in torrents, mixed with sleet. I had never done this before and I was the first to step out of the tent in my tighty-whities, camp clogs and nothing else. Since it was both shocking and invigorating at the same time, I felt it was easier to soap scrub and rinse if I screamed like a schoolgirl. I washed my hair from a five-gallon water container that sat on the tailgate of one of our trucks. Each of the other guys followed me (although I believe Bill had to pay Joe five bucks to get him to do it). Joe didn't find out until later that Bill and I giggled from the tent as we took photos of him following my example.

I had never broken down camp before in driving rain. It just wouldn't let up, but we had to get home. We put on our rain ponchos and braved the bad weather one storage tub, duffle bag and camp chair at a time, quickly loading the vehicles in a most unorganized way. Not sure why I had toweled off after my shower as water ran down my neck and also soaked my gloves, boots and pants below the knees. Finally, just as we were ready to start our muddy drive away from our campsite, the clouds broke enough for us to see that the sawtooth peaks surrounding us had a fresh dusting of snow.

We certainly had a hunting season of firsts. Unexpected adventures. Much of it like nothing we'd planned. Challenges that took us to our limits. A lot of work, at my age, without much success, as most measure success for this sport. I said I thought I was done—this would be my last hunting season.

Not long after, we were already planning for the next year's hunt.

Thwarted Yet Again

THE FOLLOWING SEASON, AND NO SURPRISE HERE, I FAILED AT hunting again. This time hunting during rifle season, or as my calls it, "hiking with a rifle."

Clearly, I'm big game's best friend. Wild critters all personally request me as a hunter for their regional mountain area, knowing that my clumsy, heavy-footed presence in their forest home surely guarantees their safety. The closest I got to even seeing game was the butt end of one elk running away over a ridge into a thick, golden-yellow aspen grove, alerted by my crashing through brush. What a chicken. He wouldn't even stand and fight like a man...er, wapiti.

I understand that not everyone shares my passion for the sport of hunting. That's okay. For those more compassionate toward the elk than me, I need to tell you that my wife said of the hunt this time (after years of crushing frustration), "Come back with freezer meat for winter, or don't come back at all." Seems a little harsh. Who needs the sympathy now?

So I tried again. I was off the grid for a few days, away from the civilized world, into the wild, again in the Uncompahgre National Forest, deep in the dark woods. I was up each morning well before dawn, and hiked for miles following game trails, hunting rifle over my shoulder, trail snacks in my pack. This time it was personal. It was me or the bull elk—one of us was not coming out alive. Perhaps a bit melodramatic, but you have to admire my determination, if not my hunting skills.

When I returned home, empty handed—surprised by a forgiving, warm welcome—I posted on my blog site stunning photos of aspen-ringed Rowdy Lake in the Big Cimarron Valley. What will you *NOT* see in that picturesque setting? The answer: *ANY* elk. I found out from a trip into town for ATV repair parts that all the elk once there (other than the one coward I saw) were at a sports bar miles away in the town of Montrose for the Broncos football game.

I'm not too discouraged, however. To be honest, I'm hunting more for scenic photo opportunities anyway. And some stories. I found plenty of each. Although, tough to fill the freezer with those. Rowdy Lake was beautiful. Maybe I should have brought my fishing pole rather than my hunting rifle.

Raining on Our Parade (er, Hunt)

Life is filled with enough disappointments. Why must I deliberately add more categories—like hunting—to fail in? Am I actually looking for success, in the failure department?

Here I was again, one more time. One more year. No one was forcing me to go out into the wilderness, get up at 3 a.m., get dressed and grab my bow (yes, pursuing that fantasy again), stumble through the forest in the dark, slosh through marshes and streams, sit on a log and cramp up by a game trail (with the vain *hope* that some beasty might mosey by), and then walk for hours back to camp in driving rain. I choose this.

For Joe and Bill (returning, as well, for more punishment), this weekend held as much promise, and mistaken vision, as other season openers. In our minds and plans, we would see game, bugle in a big bull elk to fight for the ladies, "bag" it, and have bragging rights to match other successful hunters we know. Right.

I will say this: If we were going to strike out again, we could not have selected a more beautiful place to do it. This deep-cut valley with steep slopes up to jagged mountains, by Silver Jack Lake, in the San Juan Mountains, is quite a spectacular setting. When out in the woods, trying to think and act like elk, and predator, we were enjoying the scenery as much as the thrill of the hunt. That was until the storm came ... and didn't leave.

Afternoon thunderstorms are expected for Colorado summers. But what I've loved in the past about archery season during the month of September is that the weather is a little cooler, the fall leaves are turning yellows, oranges, and reds, and typically you can count on it *not* to rain every afternoon. Not this year. It rained, and it rained, and it rained. And then it rained some more. No elk in its sound mind—or even with chronic wasting disease—would be walking around in these torrents. Not like us!

Soaking wet from head to toe, we staggered into camp after dark. At least we'd be able to get out of the weather into our dry tent, change into fresh clothes, have a simple dinner and climb into our warm sleeping bags. Well … guess who left the tent window flap open and the front door unzipped for ventilation? (Hey, it wasn't supposed to rain this late in September!) Our sleeping bags were wet, our jackets soaked, even our camp pillows were damp (the horror!). We couldn't even get around in socks, as the tent floor was flooded. We did the best we could to hunker down for a while in the truck cab, munched on P, B, and J sandwiches, and tried to dry things out with the heater and defroster on high.

It continued to pour, with high winds whipping around the tent at times, keeping us awake most of the long night. And it was still raining in the morning, dampening our spirits. We called it quits a day early. The elk beat us again—this time aided by foul weather.

But we'll be back the next year, I suppose. And we'll try once again, despite my whining, complaining, and "I'll never do that again" attitude. This will surprise no one who has ever hunted. That's the funny thing about hunting: It's about hope, anticipation, dreams, and opportunity for accomplishment at *something*. With hunting, rain or shine, success or failure, there is always another try. One more chance for achievement. Life in general doesn't always offer that.

Chapter Thirty-Two
TINY STALKER

"Cats don't need to be possessed; they're evil on their own."—Peter Kreeft

EMERALD VALLEY RANCH, PIKE NATIONAL FOREST, COLORADO

I HAD SURVIVED my first seasonal position pulling solo duty as a Winter Caretaker for the Broadmoor Hotel's regional wilderness camps in Colorado. I'm happy to report that despite such isolated settings, I did not get torn to pieces by wild animals. I rotated through three beautiful mountain properties, and I was privileged to be able to work and write in such scenic locales. Much of this book was organized, and the stories edited, in lodges or cabins at these picturesque and inspirational sites.

At the start of my second week at one of the camps, Emerald Valley Ranch, I had my first encounter with wildlife, a barn cat named June Bug. That day, long afternoon shadows were soon to give way to dusk on the forested grounds. Night came quickly to the valley. The last of the sunlight on Gray Back Peak to the east reminded me of the golden-orange alpenglow I often see on mountain summits when I start my trail hiking early in the morning. A light breeze stirred the pine branches. Here she came, casting her own long, ominous shadow. Sure, to some she would appear cute and innocent. But a closer look revealed the face of a determined predator. If she wasn't so diminutive, and aware of that fact, I'm sure I'd be dinner.

I can't say I dislike cats (okay, maybe a little bit), but typically I keep my distance. In full disclosure, I am highly allergic to the little felines. I learned this early on in life by putting precious, fuzzy kittens up near my young face, only to suffer for days with violent sneezing and viewing the world through watery, swollen eyes. In my encounters with cats through the years, it seems as though they can smell my fear and are attracted to me like catnip. I'd keep my eye on this one—a cat so eager, when guests are at the ranch, to uncharacteristically avail herself of people's food or their cabin pillows in the evenings.

Morning and night, whether doing my rounds, checking cabins or flinging hay and horse manure, I was followed. I would walk down a path, and there she'd be, watching me from behind a post. I'd be sweeping or mopping inside a building, and I'd hear her mewing, trying to draw me out into her world. I'd see cat prints in the snow leading back to my caretaker cabin. Once inside, I'd see her looking at me through the window. Obviously, her goal was to drive me insane, kill me somehow (she's still devising a plan in her dark, little Cat Cave), and eat me one tiny cat bite a time.

Lest I sound too paranoid and unreasonable, in my defense, I had recently read a revealing (and not surprising to me) article about *Felis catus* in *USA Today*, referencing a study in the *Journal of Comparative Psychology*. Sure, cat lovers think of little Mittens as charming and cuddly, but research shows domestic house cats to be neurotic, suspicious, unstable and aggressive toward humans, sharing similar characteristics with wildcat cousins like tigers, cheetahs and lions. The study from the University of Edinburgh in Scotland and the Bronx Zoo in New York concluded that if your cat was larger, it would probably consider killing you. We have invited little predators into our homes, and they *can* be sweet companions, curious, playful and impulsively funny... until they put the finishing touches on their plans to turn on you.

And then, sometime later, I read a news report on Yahoo! News, out of Tokyo, the Japanese police had opened a probe into the attempted murder of an elderly woman. The suspect? A stray cat that loitered around the poor woman's house. Ah-ha! Call me paranoid, will you!

Mayuko Matsumoto's daughter found her mother bleeding profusely from multiple cuts to her face at her home in a mountainous (uh-huh, mountainous) region of southern Japan.

"When we found her, blood covered everything above her chin," Mayuko's daughter reported. "Her face was soaked in blood. I didn't know what had happened."

Investigators found no sign of anyone entering of leaving the house at the time of the suspected attack, but did notice a cat skulking in the shadows in a corner of a room. They realized that Mayuko's wounds looked like cat scratches. At this reporting, police were analyzing blood samples taken from the claws of the cat.

Of course the cat denies any involvement in the violence against the woman, and claims that she was in a trash can in the alleyway during the time of the attack. And says she has witnesses.

Each of the weeks that I would return back to this ranch, I stayed alert and documented what I saw. I alerted friends and family that should I not come off the mountain on time, paw prints linked to foul play would be found everywhere in the snow. I instructed them to look for cat puke and fur balls on my decaying body.

Tiny Hiker

THIS CLEVER CAT—NAMED "THE STALKER" BY ME, FOR CLEAR covert actions and suspected evil intentions, details known only to her—was eventually renamed by me. "The Hiker" followed me all around on my short treks on trails surrounding the mountain property where I provide winter caretaker duties. Wherever I go, whether walking the grounds or hiking the foothills, I have a feline shadow.

My good friend at home, Sir Lancelot, or Lance the Wonder

Dog, as we call him, loves to hike with me. He thoroughly enjoys getting outdoors, into the backwoods, with the wild smells, the undomesticated environment, and the thrill of discovery. I guess most dogs do. But who knew a cat would like that too? As I said, I'm not a cat person, but I'll admit to a growing affection for this fellow hiker, a kindred spirit, enjoying the high country. How could I not feel a connection?

Not only did June Bug tail me every step along the way on my hikes, she often chose to follow the exact same route I led with. If on a trail I crossed a glistening frozen creek, stepping carefully on snow-covered rocks or a fallen log, she followed the same course I chose. If I was trudging through fresh powder, my new hiking buddy stepped in my tracks rather than making her own. She did run ahead and lead sometimes but kept looking back to see if I was staying close and if I would have picked the same direction through the forest. The bit of bouldering I did proved no problem for my wee four-legged furry friend.

One chilly day, we (I say *we* because I was never without my little shadow) took a great short hike just outside of the property. We pushed through six inches of fresh powder near a frozen creek up the a trail towards Nanny's Cabin (or what's left of it). In the 1920s, the Broadmoor Hotel builder/owner, Spencer Penrose, took guests up into the mountains behind the hotel to Emerald Valley Ranch (Penrose's hunting camp, then called Camp Virgil, after the mountain in close proximity). As many as 100 guests would be invited to dinner. After the meal, the children would be taken by horse and buggy to Nanny's Cabin as the adults danced to a full orchestra late into the evening. A bit of the original stone foundation, and most of the fireplace still exist, as well as the memories of times gone by. At a certain point, June Bug did turn back while I pressed on. My concerns about the cat making it back to the ranch proved unfounded when I fed her a kitty-food breakfast the next morning in her warmed room at the horse stables.

Now, I'm still not saying that this cat—if she could, given the research about her kind—would still not like to murder and devour me. She could have reconsidered, given our recognized relative size difference. Perhaps June Bug has simply decided she has grown to enjoy my company in turn. In any case, I've taken her off my personal tiny terrorist list. I will give her the benefit of a doubt that she simply enjoys hiking as much as I do.

Oh, sure, she's cute and everything ... but I'm still not turning my back on her.

Chapter Thirty-Three
BARKING UP THE RIGHT TREE

"Learn character from trees, values from roots, and change from leaves."—Tasneem Hameed

VARIOUS FOREST HIKES, COLORADO

AS CLEVER AND perceptive as I think I am trail hiking through the woods and capturing life lessons from the wilderness, many have gone before me and have recorded some delightful insights. When I see a pine tree that has survived a lightning strike, its bark burned and scarred, a large cut running down its trunk, I tend to take a more pragmatic approach to how I might take impressions back to my work-a-day life back home.

Novelist John Fowels speaks of the woods perhaps a bit more ethereal than my thoughts on what I've observed: "In some mysterious way, woods have never seemed to me to be static things. In physical terms, I move through them; yet in metaphysical ones, they seem to move through me."

I'm a simple guy that sees simple things in a simple way, and, simply speaking, comes to simple conclusions. I think nature, in all its wonderful complexities, often delivers illustrations for living in simple ways to those with eyes open. So I appreciate the practicality of the metaphor singer/songwriter Dolly Parton wrote: "Storms make trees take deeper roots." That I can relate to.

Although not as deep as Fowels, nor as poetic as Parton, below I offer three trees I encountered and impressions I derived on trails in the woods.

Now That's an Effort

ON A GAME TRAIL IN THE UNCAMPHAGRE NATIONAL FOREST A few years ago, something caught my attention. Not far from a small creek, a young pine tree had gotten knocked down, some time ago it seemed. It happens. Maybe by wind, a snow slide, mud at the bank giving loose, or clobbered by another tree, banged down itself by some unknown force. A domino effect perhaps.

This sapling could have thrown in the needles and just given up. It could have just stayed where it landed, on the ground, roots embarrassingly exposed, stripped of some of its branches, withered up with time and died. That's life. What was the point anyway? There were plenty of other evergreens in the dense forest, most taller, fuller, far healthier. This tree would not be known, would not make a difference, would not matter. It would have not been the shelter to birds in a thunderstorm. Would not have provided pine nuts to noisy squirrels. Would not have been shade to a hunter napping beneath mid-day.

But what an amazing thing had happened. The will to live, to grow, to thrive. To compete for space in a crowded woodland world. To seek the light that broke through the landscape, anything upwards. This little tree couldn't turn itself upright (things would never be just the same again) but it could change directions, make the best of the cards dealt it, and try, try, try, to reach the sky.

What determination! Over time (maybe just a foot a year?) the pine had made a full U-turn off the forest floor and was again striving to grow to a higher place. It didn't just resign itself to its plight, but fought for life, for meaning, for purpose. I wish I could see that tree in a hundred years, seeing its thick bent trunk at its base, knowing just part of its story. But admiring its tremendous effort.

Cool on the Outside

I'VE SEEN THIS MANY TIMES IN MY HIKES AROUND THE STATE OF Colorado, in the forests, on the trees. I saw it again on my hike on Segment 27 of the Colorado Trail in the San Juan Mountains.

It looks kinda cool—a bit like something out of a primeval scene from a *Lord of the Rings* movie. Very eerie and atmospheric. The moss hangs like a beard on the pines. Sometimes it even looks like hairy, mint-colored Christmas icicles, when drenched by an afternoon rainstorm. Pretty in a way; disturbing in another.

The trees that this wispy stuff drapes off of are dead, or dying. But it's not the fault of this moss-like lichen just looking for a place to hang out. It's not a parasite; it arrived late to the funeral. It often grows on sick or dead trees due to the preexisting loss of canopy leaves or needles, allowing now greater photosynthesis for the Spanish moss-like plant.

Usnea laponica is the scientific name for several species of lichen that generally grow hanging from tree branches. It is referred to as Old Man's Beard, Beard Lichen, Tree's Dandruff, A Woman's Long Hair, or simply Tree Moss. When a tree is clothed in the lichen, it does have a certain otherworldly beauty about it.

I could not help but think if I sometimes present a cool-looking exterior (without a green beard), but I am sick beneath. Cool on the outside; dead on the inside. I guess I need to just keep reaching higher, and try to keep my inner spirit healthy, well grounded, with roots sunk deep. Without continued life and vitality, I don't want to find myself transformed into something other than what I was meant to be.

New Life Out of Old

A BIG PINE TREE DIES AND DECAYS ON THE FOREST FLOOR. Sometimes it looks like recent deadfall, perhaps fallen (and it can't get up) that very season. More often it found its final resting place long ago and has become a rotting speed bump of its former self—a memory of a tree once standing tall, and slowly disappearing back into the soil that birthed it.

Forest conifers (pine, fir and spruce trees—with needles and cones) die for a variety of reasons. Kinda like us, I guess. Corpses lay everywhere in the forest. Some areas look like a backwoods war zone, and beg the question, "What in the world happened here?" Clues usually abound, or you might have read recorded history of the area that explains the devastation. Certainly, it's all part of nature's cycle of life. Expected. Necessary. Ultimately beneficial. But kind of sad too, thinking of the life that once tried to sink roots in deep, and reach boughs up to break out of the shadows of other trees trying to do the same.

Yet, I've seen something marvelous coming from this time and again. I even looked for it specifically (not hard to find) on one hike on the Colorado Trail. Out of the dead comes new life. I've found saplings literally growing right out of their fallen forefathers. Some out of the trace of debris, some out of the dry horizontal trunk, some right out of the uprooted foot of the tree. I've even seen new growth coming out of the middle of a stump in a age-old logged meadow.

New life out of old. We see it in the forest. We can see it played out in our lives. I am continually amazed about the life lessons from the wilderness. This example is a trade-in…or a trade up. One wise writer said it this way: "… the *old* has gone, the new has come!"

Chapter Thirty-Four
ALWAYS FALL SEASON

"Life is not about how fast you run or how high you climb, but how well you bounce."—Tigger

TARRYALL RIVER VALLEY, PIKE NATIONAL FOREST, COLORADO

I HAVE WRITTEN OFTEN about the fact that I fall down … a lot. I am both embarrassed and proud about that. Embarrassed that I trip and fall on my wilderness hikes, and then report on it. Proud that I was even out on the trails, and that I stood up after each fall, dusted myself off and didn't quit. To have survived trail falls, and to have kept going, is a badge of honor.

One of my assignments as a winter caretaker for The Broadmoor Hotel's wilderness camps was up in the Tarryall River Valley in Colorado. Appropriately called Fly Fishing Camp, this seasonal fishing property is situated on 75 acres along two miles of the Tarryall River. A beautiful setting with steep cliffs on the east side of the river, a combination of open meadows and dense pine forests, and charming fully-renovated 1920s fishing cabins, this is a lovely location to take a bad fall.

The Tarryall Creek (seasonally, a roaring river) was one of the most active locations for the prospecting of gold during the Colorado Gold Rush in 1859. The "Tarryall diggings" and other nearby sites on the east side of South Park (yes, *that* South Park) attracted thousands of prospectors. Many of the old pioneer and gold rush buildings pepper the valley—a great place for history-seeking shutterbugs. In my opinion, the whole valley should be designated a National Historic Site.

In 1955, Rory Calhoun, later of the CBS TV series *The Texan*, and actress Julie Adams co-starred in a film titled *The Looters*, the fictional story of a plane crash in the Rocky Mountains. The movie was filmed around the Tarryall River Valley. The advertising poster for the not-so-blockbuster read: "Five desperate men ... and a girl who didn't care ... trapped on a mountain of gale-lashed rock!" Sounds like a typical week for me at camp. But I digress.

Before my slip-up, or slip on, it had already been a challenging day. This camp is very secluded, about two hours into the mountains from Colorado Springs, and I was on my own to provide security, daily chores, light maintenance and repairs, and regular reporting to the home base. I was very comfortable with the isolation as I do a lot of solo hiking in the wilderness. But with today's technologies, at the camps, I had creature comforts and several ways to communicate to the outside world —except this morning, when I lost all power. I didn't know if this complication was limited to the camp property or extended to the whole valley. I already had no cell phone in the deep, narrow valley. But now, I had no lights, no computer, no Web connection or Wi-Fi, no land line, no ability text or FaceTime on my iPhone, and no receiver power for the long-distant walkie-talkie.

In the middle of winter, I now had no heat either. This didn't seem too much of a problem. The caretakers who rotated through the three properties were required to be self-sufficient in any unexpected circumstance. I felt like a real western pioneer. I had gas lamps and flashlights. I could start a blazing fire in the lodge's stone fireplace and could pull the Adirondack-style couch close for warmth. I had also brought my zero-degree sleeping bag with me (something the pioneers didn't have!). I could wait this out if I had to. It would be an adventure.

Even with these inconveniences, it still didn't seem like it would be quite as bad as the month before, when I lost my water supply for three days due to frozen pipes at the lodge, where the caretaker quarters are located. I had to boil snow for water to drink and flush the toilet. As you may know—and I was painfully reminded—it takes about 10 inches of snow to boil down to about one inch of water! And I had to filter it after that—snow, as it turns out, it not quite as pure as the driven snow. I repeatedly would have three giant cooking pots going on the stove to melt the snow I had scooped up outside. It takes a surprisingly large amount of water to flush a toilet!

One of my responsibilities at the fishing camp was to check all the cabins and the garage-barn twice a day for any evidence of winter weather damage or critters who had visited the interiors. For 11 of the 12 days at this assignment, I had carefully crossed this little bridge over a frozen tributary stream a number of times on my way back and forth to the barn. I was always cautious on the snow and ice at the camps, but especially at the fishing camp. It is the most remote of the three and had the most challenging ice flow conditions.

This was, in no small part, because a culvert under the road that parallels the property had completely frozen up. When the snow would melt on warmer days, the water would cascade over the road, flow down on to our dirt driveway, and continued on to the edge of the barn. Everything would then freeze overnight, and the pattern would continue until an ice slick about 40 yards wide blocked my access to the barn.

I found that if I cut wide, down toward the frozen river, I could bypass most of this ice flow. The little wood bridge was about half covered with ice, but I had successfully negotiated it by mostly staying on the dry part. The wilderness lesson here was never take anything for granted, and never get complacent.

In stepping from an icy part to a clear part on the bridge, my left foot slipped out from under me, and in a mico-second, I was flat on my back. I lay there for a few minutes in the dusk. I immediately hurt all over, but just how bad was this?

I willed myself to stand up on shaky legs. Everything had happened so fast, I didn't even remember hitting the ice. It was hard to grasp why my ribs hurt, my hip ached, although I could understand why my left wrist hurt like a son-of-a-gun—coming from a natural reaction to try to brace myself for impact. I had a big jacket on and gloves, so I'd take a look at my arm when I returned to the lodge. I shambled on and finished my cabin rounds.

I WAS SO PLEASED—ESPECIALLY GIVEN MY CIRCUMSTANCES—that warm light poured out onto the veranda deck upon my arrival back at the lodge. The power had come on again. I pulled my gloves and jacket off to reveal a wrist bent at an unnatural angle, and impossibly swollen. That couldn't be right. I made a call to home base, and two hours later, my replacement arrived. In another two hours, after my one-handed drive down the mountain roads, I was awaiting X-rays in the emergency room. At 4 in the morning, I returned home with bruised ribs, hip and ego … and a badly broken wrist in a splint and a sling.

To make a short story longer, in a couple of days, my wrist was set in a cast (neon green, my wife's choice). I was back at work the next morning. Two weeks later, the doctor had me scheduled for surgery—not news I wanted to hear, but X-rays showed that the bone was slipping and not healing correctly. If not fixed, the doctor told me, I'd live the rest of my life in pain and deformity. Hmmm…tough choice, but I opted for the operation, which I knew would put the recovery time that much farther out. What in the world did the western pioneers, gold miners or Rory Calhoun do with an accident like this? Glad I didn't have to find out.

The Cat and the Cast

THREE DAYS AFTER MY SURGERY—A PLATE INSERTED WITH NINE screws (the doctor said he discovered the damage was worse than he first thought)—and a new cast, I returned to my caretaker duties. Humpty Dumpty was put back together. I was back at Emerald Valley Ranch, the property that some readers on

Facebook called "Kitty Camp" because of my reporting on June Bug, the barn cat. In fact, as many followed the stories from that camp, more people asked about how June was doing than inquired about me. She had taken on legendary and celebrity status.

Upon our meeting again that morning at the barn, while I refilled her kitty bowl with fresh kibble, Jung Bug seemed genuinely curious about my cast. Didn't she know that inquisitive interest could kill her? If that continued, she'd be down to eight lives.

This feline had evoked sympathy and affection from my Facebook friends. I can see that, but they didn't have to live with its continual, overt stalking, its cold, plotting stare, or the threatening message it left with its tiny paw prints in the snow circling my caretaker cabin. One might call it simple curiosity in what was now on my arm, but I think it looked on this as a tactical advantage. In my mind, the cat viewed this as a broken wing, which, in its tiny, delusional, predatory brain, gave it a superior position over me. Again, June Bug may have failed to recognize the obvious difference in our sizes, or that my cast could be used as a club to defend myself.

During the balance of my assignment at Kitty Camp, I continued to keep alert concerning this disingenuous friendly cat, when I could see her, when she was not peering at me through narrowed eyes from the dark shadows under cabin decks. I had broken my wrist, and that was a pain in the, well, arm, but I wasn't about to become a buffet substitute for kitty kibble.

Chapter Thirty-Five
WHAT A RUSH!

"A dream becomes a goal when action is taken towards its achievement."—Bo Bennett

CLOCKWORK CLIMBING CLUB, MT. EVANS (14,265 FT.)/MT. SHERMAN (14,035 FT.), CO

TRACY SAT DOWN ON A BOULDER, face flushed. I approached him to see how he was doing. He had struggled from the start of this high-country trail and now seemed to have reached his limit. I had been keeping a close eye on him—I can usually pick up on the early signs of dehydration and/or altitude sickness rather quickly. The latter is easy to notice. The symptoms include (any combination of) fatigue, headache, dizziness, shortness of breath, nausea and general malaise.

"I'm *really* not feeling great," Tracy said with a sigh. "I don't think I can make it … not today."

We were not very far into the climb of the 14,265-ft peak of Mt. Evans in Colorado, and the rest of our group were already stretching out a lead. We talked for a few minutes. A tough decision by Tracy, and maybe by me, needed to be made ….

❄

A COUPLE OF YEARS AGO, I HAD THE PRIVILEGE OF HELPING guide a diverse group of 15 hikers from all over the country up to the top of their very first Colorado 14er. They differed from one another in backgrounds, vocations, ages, conditioning and hiking abilities. But all were united in their fan support for the rock band Rush, as well as for my fiction writer bro-in-law, Kevin. And they were all committed to having a grand adventure on the mountain. Of course, they hoped to summit. And I would do anything I could to help them achieve that goal.

You might wonder what connects a Canadian three-man super group, a best-selling author, people from different regions (who all happen to love sci-fi and fantasy books and movies), and a massive mountain on the Front Range west of Denver. And what happened to Tracy?

As I understand it, there has always been a symbiotic relationship between progressive rock and sci-fi-fantasy books and movies. Progressive rock (or prog rock) albums have not typically featured songs that make the Top 10 radio hits. More often than not, they are full album stories, ones to be experienced from start to finish, not cherry-picked for favorite tunes, nor do the songs many times even fit the limited time allowed on the radio between commercials. The progressive rock form is often characterized by classical influences, the use a keyboard, some strings, lengthy compositions, and seems to deliberately abandon the danceable beat. Thematically, prog rock albums—with their story-telling—can take fans to realms, other worlds, other universes.

Symphonic or prog rock styles have always been favored music genres of Kevin's. He enjoys the storytelling aspect of the songs and the transport to other realms. Well, and of course, the rock 'n' roll musical aspect too. One of Kevin's favorite bands was Rush. Simply a fan, he contacted Neil Peart, Rush's lyricist and drummer extraordinaire, to express his admiration. As it turned out, Neil was a fan of Kevin's sci-fi books. Over the years, Neil and Kevin became good friends. Neil would even stay at Kevin's home as the group traveled the U. S. on a concert tour, preferring to ride his motorcycle rather than the traditional rock band tour bus. They talked often about doing a project together some day, which eventually became the *Clockwork Angels* book, a novelization of Rush's studio album of the same title.

Enter Chris Reed, a designer from Virginia, and a fan of both Kevin and Neil, who, in turn, became fans of Chris and his design projects (a lot of admiration going on here). Chris and his engineer/manufacturer/software developer friend, Jim, contacted Kevin to express their fan support, and to see if Kevin could get some beautifully designed and etched Rush drinking glasses to Neil, which Kevin did (Neil loved them). So began another friendship based on sci-fi, beer, and rock-n-roll.

Chris knew of Kevin's love of the Great Outdoors and how much he enjoyed summiting 14ers. He had also read of the account of Kevin and Neil climbing Mt. Evans in Colorado, and how they mapped out the storyline for *Clockwork Angels* along the way. He contacted Kevin about the idea of taking a group of Rush fans—mostly strangers to each other—up Evans in honor of the rock band retiring, and as a sort of "pilgrimage" up the mountain to retrace the steps Kevin and Neil took together while working out the origins and details of their best-selling book.

Kevin jumped on the idea—his only concern that the hiker-fans would be fit enough for a challenging climb like this. Once announced, the response to the opportunity was so enthusiastic, Kevin and Chris had to quickly limit the registrations. Kevin invited (strongly requested?) me to come along to help guide the group to the top. The plan was for me to hang back with the anticipated slower members, encouraging them step-by-step to keep going, or to get them safely back to the parking lot, and then I'd rejoin the others. Of course, I was all in, especially since I had climbed Mt. Evans and it's sawtooth ridge connecting the companion Mt. Bierstadt many times. Both peaks are challenging but enjoyable, and I looked forward to helping others to have a similar experience.

The night before our planned ascent, we had a meet-and-greet with the excited, first-time 14er climbers. We convened at a popular brewery-restaurant in Idaho Springs, and we all connected like we were old friends, I suppose because of all the mutual crossover interests. After all the introductions and the great dinner conversations, Kevin and I went over next-day issues which included what to expect in the morning, what to pack (we brought extra clothing and supplies for those that didn't pay attention to the many pre-hike prep emails), and general explanation of the climb and experience.

The Expedition Begins

OUR ADVENTURE STARTED PRE-DAWN WITH THE DRIVE UP THE Mt. Evans Highway. Our anticipation built with each mile we drove higher and higher to the trailhead. We broke treeline just about the time the sun broke the horizon. Despite this high country region having seen a snowstorm already (in August!), this day looked to be cool but clear.

The cast of characters piled out of several vehicles at the Summit Lake trailhead parking lot below Mt. Evans. We all layered up, found and loaded on our backpacks, grabbed our hiking sticks, and put on gloves and knit hats. It was chilly!

Kevin and I gathered the intrepid hikers together to point out our route that would take us up and around the edge of the huge bowl that surrounded the crystal-blue lake. The rich variety of new-found friends included manufacturer Jim, Chris and his young son Evan, Ronald, also from Virginia, an HVAC engineer for a school system, and his daughter, Kelly, a nurse, and John, an airline pilot for Frontier Airlines, who, obviously, was used to being at higher elevations.

Some pulled in closer to better hear the explanation about the planned adventure this day. Other than Kevin and I, none had ever summited a 14er. Anticipation was high. Others in the group included Brian, a web site developer, and his 11-year-old son Alex (Mom Tara, a proofreader for Kevin's publishing company, opted not to make the hike, but volunteered to be a pick-up driver for us, as she was terribly afraid of heights), Alex and Brandon, two dentist brothers from Denver, and Ronnie, a student and budding sci-fi/fantasy author from back east. Rounding out the band of merry men, women and boys was Elizabeth and Chris, a newly married couple from Texas, and

Warren, an FBI agent who had some wild stories to tell (those not confidential) about the work of finding and apprehending "bad guys" to keep the citizens of our country safe.

Funny story about Warren from the night before: It was a number of city blocks from our hotel in Idaho Springs to our dinner location. Being a nice evening, we all decided to walk. As our group elongated on the sidewalk, I ended up having time to chat with Warren along the way. I was curious to talk to him about his crime- fighting work in his federal job; he wanted to talk about my book, *Tales from the Trails*.

As it turned out, he had bought my first book on trail hiking experiences and really enjoyed it. He remembered every story and details from all my adventures (not surprising, being an FBI agent), both the overcoming of challenges as well as the humorous blunders. He reminisced, telling me his favorite parts from chapters in the book. It was so odd hearing someone recall stories from *my* book. Warren had me laughing out loud at my own adventures! I was both embarrassed and honored at his enthusiastic approval of my writing. But, really, laughing at your own stories … that should be a Federal crime, right?

Of course, I don't want to forget mentioning Tracy from Utah, who works at a TV news channel and volunteers to help the homeless in Salt Lake City. There just could not have been a kinder guy, with big smile and an infectious enthusiasm about life. He's the type of guy you immediately like, and everybody did. Tracy pressed in to the group, all bundled up, his face brimming with excitement, with just hint of cautious anticipation.

There are several routes to summit Mt. Evans starting around the base of the peak, and I had done most of them over the years. Kevin and I choose a course that takes you on a big, wide arc, high around the lake, across a wide saddle, and then up the back side of Evans. Any trails to the top of these 14ers are challenging, but we thought this one was well within the range of what our group could do. It was a Class 2 climbing route, still in the "beginners" category by the book. This is the same peak that I climbed with my older friend, Jim, his story in another chapter in this book, but we took a different, easier route.

I looked around at our climbing group. Nurse Kelly had turned a bit green on the curvy Mt. Evans road on the drive up —which gave us a little cause for concern—but she was able to walk it off at the parking lot. Elizabeth (who beamed at new hubby Chris, as newly-weds are prone to do) carried a much larger DSLR camera than I would recommend for a 14er summit climb, but I knew she'd record marvelous photographic memories of our adventure.

I didn't find out until later that not only had the aspiring author Ronnie never summited a 14,000-ft peak, but that he had never hiked *anywhere* before! I don't think Kevin knew that either, a key bit of information that apparently wasn't fully disclosed.

We were off! The younger ones shot out quickly on the trail to the north end of the lake, giving no thought to the importance of pacing yourself for a climb. Kevin is no help with that, with his long legs and exceptional stamina. It was cold, but we were happy that all the snow from that week had melted, as far as we could see. To our surprise, that would change at a point, making this "easier" peak a very challenging, if not somewhat dangerous climb for these beginners.

As we began to gain elevation on the east ridge of the connection to Mt. Spaulding, as expected, the group spread out, eventually clumping into two groups. And, as planned, I stayed back with the slower bunch. Just several hundred yards into the adventure, as we had to climb some rocks to gain easier terrain on the ridge, Tracy's pace slowed, and he eventually sat down on a small boulder. I sent the others on ahead to join the speedier group that Kevin led, knowing that he would pause for the slower hikers to catch up, so that everyone could move forward together on the more difficult sections ahead.

I walked back down to Tracy. He did not look well. We talked for a few minutes. Sometimes resting for a while can get a hiker up and going again. You also look to issues of hydration and fuel (some hikers just forget to keep drinking, and trail snacks, energy bars, a piece of fruit, all can give a big boost), general conditioning, and the possibility of altitude sickness. The extra body weight Tracy carried could not have helped either.

"I can get you up to the top," I offered. "I've done this many times, and with those who weren't certain they could make it."

Tracy looked down at the high alpine grass.

I continued, "We can take it slow. There is no rush—it's not a race. I'll stay with you. We'll just take it a step at a time, and we'll stop a lot and drink a lot, and have a great time along the way."

"I don't know …" Tracy answered weakly.

"It's your call," I said, "but I have gotten others up in similar situations. I know we can do this … that *you* can do this."

There is a fine line, I've discovered over the years, between being an inspirational cheerleader to those struggling up a mountain, and encouraging them on to their certain death. Hikers perish every year on 14ers, no fault of their own (loose rock, rapidly changing weather conditions), others by poor judgment, unfortunate mistakes, or being underprepared, and some simply because they really had no business being up there in the first place. I didn't want anything to happen to Tracy. Besides, having someone die on my watch on the mountain was really bad for my wilderness tour guide brand.

"What are you thinking?"

"I'm *really* not feeling great," Tracy said with a sigh. "I don't think I can make it … not today."

"Are you sure? That's perfectly okay. There's no shame in making a good judgment call like this. You can't help how you are feeling today. You can always come back another day … this mountain, or another, will still be there!"

Tracy had made the right call (and I was glad it wasn't one that I had to make for him). Together, we carefully negotiated the gravelly trail back down, walked around the edge of the lake and arrived at the car in the parking lot. With his good outlook on life, he commented that he still had a great time with everybody, and was so glad he came! I made sure he was alright to stay with the car until we all rejoined him, turned and hustled back up the trail to catch up with the others.

Once back with the group, that had like a Slinky, closed back up again, we continued up together through some rather challenging cliffy sections that required some real hand-over-foot climbing. I was so pleased to see how everyone helped everybody else, through their encouragement, and also by offering route suggestions as well as giving a hand up, or a push from behind! It was great to see a group of previous strangers so quickly becoming a supportive team.

The views looking back down on the lake were breathtaking. We all paused for photos. It wasn't until we crested the ridge at about 13,800 feet, and began to cross the long, wide saddle between Mt. Spaulding and Mt. Evans that we saw what a different world it was here at the higher elevation, and on the backside of Evans. Where we had started out from the trailhead parking lot with no snow, here, and for the rest of the climb there were several inches of snow on the trail and on rocks and boulders we had to traverse. This was unexpected and made the rest of the hike and climb quite a bit more dicey. We all had to be very cautious to not slip off a rock and twist an ankle. As you might imagine, this just made for even more of a grand adventure for our out-of-staters. Carefully negotiating what we could see of the snow-covered trail, I hung back with the delightful Virginians, dad Ronald and daughter Kelly. Their joy and enthusiasm was fun to watch, and made my experience all that more enjoyable. We still had the last mile to the summit, through the roughest of the terrain on the climb, all covered with fresh snow, and all smiles dissipated.

We closed our ranks again, after having spread out across the long saddle, looking much like an expedition trudging slow step-by-step across an Antarctic frozen wilderness. We avoided a connecting saddle to the sawtooth ridge that leads to Mt. Bierstadt (14.065 ft.) and stuck to the west side of Evans. Normally, this is just a long, steep trudge up an obvious rocky trail, with some occasional bouldering. This day, with the snow cover, it was more than slightly demanding—it was downright dangerous. This is not the climbing experience you should bring beginners on for their first 14er! What had Kevin and I done?

We all started up, staying close together, with both Kevin and I taking the lead to try to find some hints of the trail. We split up and moved forward several yards apart to see if we could discover some sign of a path. None was to be found. Even the trail direction stacked stone cairns were covered with snow. We knew, of course, that we were to go *up*, but the standard trail cut the elevation on a diagonal, making it easier to climb. We made our own trail towards the top. I tried to encourage each member that they were doing well and to just keep going. Everyone held their footing, but it was slow going and fatiguing. Chris, Jim, new-hiker Ronnie and all the rest would certainly have stories to tell when they returned home. I think Warren even stated that this was harder than anything he ever had to do in the FBI, at least that's what I remember.

The rock stars on top of Mt. Evans, already planning our next adventure.

Very close to the final push to the summit, we all paused for a break, regrouped and had a pep talk. We were almost there, but that last mile up the snow-covered boulder fields had taken its toll on some. We were all exhausted. Brian's poor young son Alex bent over a rock and blew out all his trail snacks, his breakfast, and probably everything he ate the day before. He said he actually felt a little better after emptying his stomach. He showed great courage and determination by wanting to press on to the top—an inspiration to us all.

We summited the peak, and you can imagine the elation of each member of the group. What a rush! They all had just accomplished something very special for the first time, and each did more than they thought they were capable of doing. Hugs and "high-fives" ensued, followed by the traditional group photo at the top. Chris had brought a string of Tibetan prayer flags that he had made with our new hiking club logo on it. It made our "elevation celebration" all the more colorful and festive.

All survived. Memories were made. Great friendships were forged. I'd call that a good day. Before we were back to the hotel, plans were being made for the next climb.

Fast forward one year ...

The Adventure Continues

Sure enough, what had become the Clockwork Climbing Club (with logo, Facebook member site and a secret handshake) was reunited in Colorado ready to conquer another peak. We staged in the little mountain town of Fairplay, and had our pre-climb planning dinner the night before at the South Park Brewery. Yes, *that* South Park region of the Rockies, made famous (or infamous) by Trey Parker and Matt Stone with their *South Park* animated TV series. There really is no town of South Park as a town, but Fairplay does have a little historic South Park outdoor museum with relocated pioneer-day buildings to walk around, for an admission price. Fairplay has done a good job of promoting itself through coopting the cartoon brand for business signage and tourist souvenirs.

Nearly everyone from the previous year had returned for more punishment, er, joyful adventure, to try to climb up a monster mountain. We were short one aspiring author, Evan was replaced by Chris' older son, Ethan, the Texas newly-wed couple and the two Denver dentists, but had added Warren's (he of the retelling of serious FBI stories, and the hilarious tales from my book) son and daughter, James and Mellissa. And guess who also returned? Tracy was back for another 14er summit attempt. He was no less enthusiastic about life, but leaner, and even more determined to summit a fountener.

Tracy had told me at the Mt. Evans trailhead parking lot that he'd be back, and here he was! He had worked all year to get in better condition. He ate more healthy foods. He entered and ran (walking at first) 5K and 10K races for charity events. This guy was serious! He had toned up, gained more endurance and stamina, and eventually lost over 35 pounds. He was ready to tackle one of these high-alpine beasts again. But even seasoned athletes in excellent health, from other sports, can struggle at elevation. Altitude sickness shows no favorites, is unpredictable, ignores conditioning, and can hit one person at one time and not another. Despite Tracy's hard work to get here, he'd be tested by the mountain the next morning.

Our choice of a 14er this time was Mt. Sherman (14,036 ft.) in the Mosquito Mountain Range above Fairplay, another of the "easier" Class 2 categories. I had climbed Sherman a number of times, in fact, this was my very first 14er summit with my son, Cary, when he was 14 years old. We were snowed out the morning of our first attempt, but came back two weeks later to top it. It really is one of my favorites because of the many interesting mining ruins that you pass on the way to the base of the mountain.

The enthusiastic climbers started out just after dawn from the trailhead parking area at about 12,000 feet. As expected, in less than a mile into the nearly 5-1/2 mile round trip, the group split into two fractions, shall we say kindly, those wishing to expend their energy quickly and those pacing themselves. With the same planning as before, I stayed back with the slower group. Tracy started out strong, determined, and he looked well, buoyant. He hiked with the slower group, perhaps out of caution, acutely reminded of his difficulties the previous year.

Our plodding team included Brain, wife Tara (yes, *that* Tara, she of the heights phobia) and young son Alex. Tara was going to try it this time, pushing through her fears! Each step higher and higher, it seemed as if she was dragging boulder of doubt, but she kept going. Surprisingly, it was Alex who—from the very start of the trailhead—wrestled with the mountain more than the others. One foot after the other (with many rest stops, some sitting, some fully lying down) we encouraged him slowly up the trail to a high plateau. To distract him from his focus on his struggles, I pulled out every factoid I had about the region, pointed out interesting mining relics, and told him of my own challenges on different 14ers. Even Tracy jumped it to let Alex know that he knew he could make it. We tag-teamed with Alex all the way to the massive ruins of Hilltop Mine. Tara kept climbing.

We tried to keep Kevin and his group in our sights, following his route, knowing he'd stop and let us catch up. This is typically pretty easy as Kevin usually wears hiking clothes that are very bright—a fluorescent orange cap, jacket or backpack. I think he could be seen from space. I picked up a bouncing orange ball with other hikers cutting a diagonal across a steep section on the way to the plateau. I assumed this was Kevin pack, although this was not the traditional route that I had taken many times. Our group followed the same trail not wanting to get too far behind.

Kevin wrote this account in his blog site: "We spread out as we climbed, and puffed, and panted, at our own pace. Gradually, the group separated into faster hikers and the slower hikers. I led the first pack, while Tim shepherded the others. We climbed a relentless trail, up to another set of high mining ruins—an amazing and extensive operation, which made us all wonder about the thriving settlement from more than a century ago. The faster hikers waited, trying to spot the rest of the group with Tim, Tracy, Tara, Brian and Alex, but we couldn't find them even though we could see the dirt road that was the trail for miles behind us. Did they turn back? We couldn't get a cell signal, couldn't stay in touch. We waited, but saw no sign of them, and finally pushed on. I was rooting for Tracy, hoping he hadn't suffered altitude sickness again, and for Tara to see how far she could climb, but they were far behind. We were sure they had given up and gone back to the car to wait for us."

Unknown to Kevin, we continued to climb upward. This route got steeper and more rocky. I couldn't figure out why Kevin had taken his group up this way. Because of the more challenging, steeper terrain, Alex had to stop more, and Tara was starting to show some real, perhaps justified anxiety. At 12,800 feet, near the Hilltop Mine building, we joined Kevin and his group.

I pulled Kevin aside and whispered, "Why did you take that more difficult route up?"

"I didn't," he said, "We took the standard route." He pointed to the wide, gentle trail off to his left. "Why did you guys go up that way? That looked a lot harder!"

"I was following you—your bright orange pack!"

I light bulb went on and I realized that there were of two neon-glowing hikers on the mountain this day.

We shared this with the combined groups and all had a good laugh. But I assumed those that I had mislead so badly had lost all trust in me as their seasoned guide. My slow-poke band actually beamed with pride that they had taken the more difficult route and conquered it! Yup, nailed it! We da champs!

After quick energy snacks and hydration, we were off again. We would have liked to explore around the old mine building, but we had the toughest part of our climb still ahead of us. We crossed a large, relatively flat area, then began to climb up to the 13,150-ft. saddle between Mt. Sheridan and Mt. Sherman. From here, the trail got much steeper and more rocky.

Warren's teens, James and Mellissa, shot up the trail like mountain goats (with Dad *mostly* keeping up). Oh … for youth again. Tracy was doing great, and I told him so, having no doubts that he'd make it to the top. Up, up, up we climbed, working our way over boulders, finding the sketchy trail when we could, at other times, connecting the dots by following the stacked rock cairns.

Staying back with the slower group, I became concerned for

Alex and mom Tara, and kept a close eye on them. Alex was really fading. 12-year-olds don't always want to take advice, even from those with a bit more experience. You can lead boy to energy snacks and water, but, apparently, you can't force them to ingest. Well, I could, but that would be terribly inappropriate, if not some kind of criminal act. Tara was understandably looking more and more anxious the higher we climbed. She was so brave and trying so hard to push beyond her fear of heights ... and this was higher than she'd ever been!

With much prodding from Mom and Dad Brian, we did finally get some fuel and hydration into Alex and he came back alive again, so to speak. It was at this point that Tracy really stepped up.

"I'll help you get to the top, Alex."

Alex looked up to Tracy's broad smile.

"We'll work together, help each other, and have 'high fives' at the summit. Okay?" Tracy asked.

Alex nodded in agreement. The guy with huge heart and big ambitions, who was disappointed he could not make the climb the previous year and had to turn back, was now assisting another to the top!

I looked back at Tara. Her face said it all. She was struggling, pushing beyond her limits. Not physically, but wrestling with fear. What an effort!

Slowly, carefully, we continued up. When we reached a narrow ridge at about 13,600 feet, requiring some real hand-over-foot climbing, Tara stopped. She said she was done, pleased about her accomplishment, but that was as far as she was going this day. I told her that we could take it slow, one step at a time, and that we could get her to the top. She was ready to go back down, and I had to respect that. We were all so proud of what Tara was able to do ... she didn't have to summit to gain our admiration. Hubby Brian accompanied her back to the trailhead parking area while I went on to join the others.

I caught up with Alex and Tracy (he had got him almost to the top) and when we together climbed over a false summit. The rest of the group was waiting for us so we could all reach the top at the same time. We ascended the much more gentle, but long, south ridge. We stopped about 1/4 mile from the true summit for me to point out an interesting aspect of this mountain top: Mt Sherman is the only Colorado 14er where an airplane has actually crash landed.

One January day in 1967, Pilot Jimmy Williamson of Denver was forced by severe down drafts in a brutal storm to use the high plateau just off the summit as an unexpected landing field. I pointed that area out to the group. Williamson was flying a Cessna 310 for a Clinton Air Charter en route to Aspen when he had to make a dramatic decision. He was able to bring the aircraft to rest in deep snow, the only possible place that made sense. His four passengers suffered only minor injuries—and what a story they had to tell: landing a plane on the top of a 14er! The bitter weather thwarted rescue efforts for 20 hours, until helicopter pilot Bob Green of Broomfield plucked the group from the peak.

Our commercial pilot John surveyed the rugged terrain and tried to create in our imaginations what that must have looked and felt like. He described what the weather and wind patterns may have been like, what would have been going through the pilot's mind at the time, and the quick thinking and tough decisions he had to make. Even though I didn't know the exact location where the plane went down, John agreed that the flat area just off the summit is where the pilot must have crashed.

At the top, we all had "high fives" and hearty back pats, and congratulatory hugs with Tracy and Alex. Both had worked so hard to push through personal obstacles. They pressed on and simply wouldn't quit. Tracy had "run the race," this time up a mountain, and crossed the finish line with pride and exhilaration.

AT OUR CELEBRATION DINNER IN FAIRPLAY, AT MILLONZI'S Restaurant (yes, unexpected fine dining in "South Park"), all were shown honor in some way for their accomplishment, and each received a certificate. Tara received an additional Special Courage award for climbing higher than she'd ever been. Tracy was recognized for his year-long hard work to get back on a mountain, and for his success at summiting. Chris and Jim had made Kevin and me commemorative Mt. Sherman etched glass beer pints. And Chris presented us with a large customized color poster (that everyone signed to show appreciation) of "South Park," with both of us illustrated as the TV series characters, with me pictured with my hiking stick and dressed in my traditional green windbreaker, tan hiking pants and black, broad-brimmed hat. It looked just like me ... well, the cartoon representation, a little shorter and fatter (I think)! Still, I was very appreciative and honored.

I can't wait to go on our next adventure with these fine folks. These guys are *rock* stars!

Chapter Thirty-Six
YOU DO HOODOO?

"See the world. It's more fantastic than any dream."—Ray Bradbury

INDIAN PAINT MINES INTERPRETIVE PARK, CALHAN, COLORADO

A FEW YEARS ago was able to get out to hike on New Year's Day, early in the morning, before a rapidly approaching storm dropped about a foot of snow. It's hard to believe that after living here more than 25 years, I'm still finding trails in the Pikes Peak Region that I've never done before, especially gems like the Indian Paint Mines approximately 30 miles east of Colorado Springs.

Seems that this place is a well-kept secret—you won't find it listed as one of the "best places to see" in the tourist brochures or region websites. But, shhhh … that's just the way I like it. I was completely alone except for the occasional rabbit startled by the crunching of my boots on the snow from a recent storm.

The Paint Mines Interpretive Park is in an unexpected hollow that's cut from the otherwise rolling high plains of eastern El Paso County. The rip in the prairie land opens up to four miles of serpentine trails featuring spectacular displays of hoodoos, caprock formations, overhangs, sculpted walls, gullies and brightly colored clay deposits. Hoodoos (besides being a really funny name) are oddly shaped pinnacles or columns of weathered rock. They create a fantastical, otherworldly landscape like something from a sci-fi or fantasy movie. I had seen hoodoos when hiking around Moab, Utah, but nothing like this in Colorado.

Fantastical formations with funny names.

Named for the colorful clay striations—bands of yellows and oranges, grays, tans, rose pink and purplish mauve—the park is quite striking and looks like it was designed by Disney Imagineers on peyote. Native Americans used the deposits for ceremonial paints and pottery. Euro-American settlers in the 1800s mined the clay to make bricks for buildings in Colorado Springs and Pueblo.

The spires and hoodoos look like solid rock, but these formations are actually quite fragile. An information brochure with map and park rules is available at the small parking lot entrance. I tried to follow all the rules. I didn't remove, destroy or disturb any of the features (I wasn't even impolite to any of them). I didn't bring in any alcoholic beverages (little early in the morning for that). I didn't discharge firearms or paintball guns, nor did I set off fireworks or explosives (although, tempting).

If I did break a park rule, it may have been the one about staying on the designated trails. With the snow cover, I probably strayed a bit, uncertain exactly where the trail was. We'll keep that our little secret.

Chapter Thirty-Seven
FOOL ON A HILL

"Life is too short to be serious all the time. So, if you can't laugh at yourself, call me … I'll laugh at you."—Unknown (but I have a few suggestions)

TOP OF CHEYENNE MOUNTAIN, PIKE NATIONAL FOREST, COLORADO

I HAD BEEN FOLLOWING the weather reports all week. A monster spring storm was coming, the only question was just how big. One forecaster said snow accumulation could be somewhere between 5 and 50 inches. That was helpful.

I was up doing my caretaker responsibilities at the mountaintop camp (not the valley property with the barn cat) and didn't know how this storm would affect me. Cloud Camp is at 9,200 feet above Colorado Springs on top of Cheyenne Mountain, so I was certain I'd get clobbered. I had no vehicle, so I was going to be stuck no matter how bad the storm.

I wonder what story might come out of this, I thought. As it turned out … well, I think I'll let my Facebook posts, and response from friends and family tell the tale. (Note, I've left off the posted photos and links.)

❄

Timothy Jones
Friday, April 15 6:24 pm

Post: Yup. It's started. Heavy, wet, white stuff. 24 inches now forecasted. Doubt I will be getting off the mountain this weekend. In short sleeves yesterday at 9,200 feet. Gotta love Springtime in Colorado!

[I posted photos of start of snowfall]

Kathy Incredible! (from Southern California)

Jane All I can say is, "Oh boy."

Me Mom, that's all you can say?

Vina I miss the kitty!

Me LOL! I'll update everyone about the barn cat June Bug when I start driving guests to the ranch first of May! That cat is a celebrity now!

That cat gets more inquiries, attention and affection than I do!

Ann Oh, how well we remember shoveling snow off the deck in the spring in Lake City, Colorado. One year we even had snow on the 4th of July. Could never plant until after Father's Day. It is called the joys of living at 9,500-ft altitude. LOVED EVERY MINUTE OF IT!

Tina Craaaaazzzzyyyyy!!!!!!!

Me That was a real crazy "Crazy!" Love the enthusiastic response!

Timothy Jones
Saturday, April 16 11:50 am

Post: Step back, people. Just back away … no Colorado wilderness to see here today. Nothing to see, go home. Or stay home.

[I posted a photo looking out the lodge window, nothing but complete whiteout conditions]

Me Hope I have enough food to last out the storm. Didn't plan to have to stay extra days out here on this caretaking assignment.

Mom Always an adventure or pickle you get yourself into!!! So far you have been handling it okay. Hope you have enough to eat.

Me I found myself thinking about gnawing on my own paw a few minutes ago, but good sense got the better of me. I'm going back to boiling old shoe leather for dinner.

Mom Hear the bears are out of hibernation. Be careful, they are hungry also.

Me And thanks for the bear reminder, on top of everything else.

Sydna Glad June Bug isn't there, or you may think of eating her, huh?

Me You cat lovers won't like my response! But in a survival situation … hmmm … Vietnamese stir-fry, warm kitty fur gloves, cat's eye marbles, and a trophy cat-tooth necklace? Hey, I watch "Survivorman" on TV. Anyway, with June Bug, you never know … could eat her, or be eaten by her.

Mom Run, June Bug, run!

Me (posted image of a laughing-hard emojicon)

Sydna You just like to shock us all, don't you, Tim? Let's hope it never comes to that or I think June Bug might be the victor!

Timothy Jones
Saturday, April 16 5:04 pm

Post: Don't even know how much snow has accumulated here at camp on Cheyenne Mountain, and the drifts are ridiculous—maybe three feet. I wouldn't send a dachshund out in this to do his business … wouldn't find him until summer.

[I posted a photo looking out the caretaker bedroom window at two-foot long icicles, with snow drifts halfway up the windows]

Kathy No words other than YIKES!

Nothing else? No other words?

Me Whaaaat? It's not like this in Southern California right now?

Mom Burr!

Me It's starting to look like something out of the movie *Doctor Zhivago* up here.

Mom But at least he had a companion.

Jim We got to do this today: (photo of family kayaking on lake, Bremerton, Washington)

Marilyn Great pics! Was 80 degrees at the Dodger's game today.

Sydna WOW! It's near 80 degrees here today (Fayetteville, Arkansas)

Thank you all for reminding where I DON'T live.

Timothy Jones
Saturday, April 16 5:48 pm

Post: THERE IS NO EXIT FOR ME OFF THIS SNOWY mountain, that is, until they plow the road Monday morning.

[I posted a photo of the EXIT sign over the door, zero visibility outside]

Mom Hang in there. Well what else can you do?

Me I've taken up needlepoint and interpretive dancing.

Timothy Jones
Sunday, April 17 9:00 am

Post: LET'S TRY THIS WINDOW FOR VIEWS OFF THE DECK. Nope. No better. Still snowing.

[I posted a photo from a different window, same bleak views]

Les Sorry, it's in the 70s in Chicago!

Me Les—why would you want to torment me, especially on

the Lord's Day. Chicago, you say? Well, at least no one is shooting at me up here in the mountains.

Les You make a very good point!

Sunday, April 17 1:00 pm

Mark View of Cheyenne Mountain from my neighborhood. I pity anyone up on top today!

[He posted a photo looking up at cloud-shrouded Cheyenne Mountain from the valley of Colorado Springs]

Me Yup, that's me up there that you *can't* see! Thick fog mixed with light flurries. Darn, I may not get outside today to snow shovel acres of drifts we have here.

Another Kathy April showers bringing May flowers here in Oklahoma City. April blizzards in your neck of the woods. LOL!

LOL? I'm not laughing at all.

Anne Are you starting to feel like Jack Nicholson in *The Shining* now?

Me "Heeeere's Timmy?"

[I posted a photo of frozen Jack Nicholson in snow from movie. Caption: "Visit Colorado in April," they said. "It'll be fun," they said.]

Timothy Jones
Sunday, April 17 4:30 pm

Post: Stuck on Cheyenne Mountain until the road is plowed. There are worse places to be cloistered for a few days. I have one day of food left. Someone ate all the emergency MREs —not me! That person needs to be fired!

[I posted an afternoon photo of the lodge from the Fire Tower Cabin, and snow-covered pines]

Diane Very nice. Breathtaking scenery … but I need you home.

Merrie Yikes. I'm starting to think you live in the Land of Perpetual Winter.

Me Yeah, it's like something on the other side of the Wardrobe! I'm in Narnia!

Kevin Sorry, I meant to send that last post to someone else, but I got distracted imagining you all alone ... with no food ... in the snow ... and thinking about the Donner Party ....

Me I have a Donner Party cookbook. The only problem is there is nobody here but me.

[I posted a photo of Donner Party cookbook]

Colleen Is it Pizza Hut that says it will deliver anywhere, anytime?

Sydna Can someone send you a drone with more food?

Marilyn That is so sad. Maybe you can have Hansel and Gretel over for dinner. Put cookies and candy on your eaves for enticement?

Or the pizza delivery guy.

Mark I'm looking for you on the website capture of the live camera feed from the Fire Tower cabin.

Me There's a live video feed from the Fire Tower camera? Dang. There goes naked Wednesdays.

Timothy Jones
Sunday, April 17 6:30 pm

Post: Well, it just won't stop. Pretty, however. Until I have to start shoveling it.

[I posted a nighttime photo of the lodge deck covered in two feet of snow]

Molly They don't give you a snowblower or a snowplow vehicle?

Me Just a nice bright-orange snow shovel. I don't think they know just how old I am, and I'm not telling them.

Ashley LOL!

I'm saying funny things?

Marc There is a leaf blower in the basement.

Molly Just go down in the basement and get the leaf blower. Now. In the dark. I'm sure there's nothing down there waiting for you. No cats. No bears.

Timothy Jones
Monday, April 18 7:00 am

Post: Well, now I've done it. Unbelievable. Stranded on the mountain, and I have gone through all the rest of my food this morning—no self-control or discipline to spread the reserves out more—and this See's candy sucker is all I have left until I'm rescued.

[I posted a photo of my laptop computer on the side table with empty cup of coffee and an unopened See's sucker]

Sydna Well, you can stand to lose some weight!

Julie There's probably an app that will show how many licks of that sucker you need per hour to make it last long enough.

Jim Wait. What happened to the CAT?!!!!

Me Hmmmm....

Sharon Don't go there. Throwing up hair balls guaranteed.

Julie ... and you have toothpaste you can eat too, right?

Adrienne Drink a lot of water! You can do it!

Me If the pipes don't freeze. Well, I always have what's left in the unflushed toilets in the rooms at the lodge.

[I posted a photo of a dog drinking out of the toilet]

Diane About that sucker, don't suck it all gone in one day. Save some for tomorrow if you need to.

Me Too late. That would have been a bit of good advice to have gotten a lot SOONER!

Sharon Do you have the makings of snow ice cream? You have at least the main ingredient.

Rocky The archery gear is downstairs in the basement, and I hear that bears are coming out of hibernation.

The bear warnings again. Sigh ...

Me Thanks, Rocky. I shutter thinking about that bear scene from the movie *The Revenant*, snacking on poor Leo.

Ruth You could always eat a limb.

Sharon Tim, you can find help online for just about anything. I found something for you to make a meal on!

[I posted a photo of ice cubes on a plate. Caption: Finally setting down to my vegan, gluten free, soy free, antibiotics free, non GMO, organic, fat free, low carb meal!]

Me Ha-ha! Too funny! Wait ... that's looking pretty good right now.

Me I tried it with some salt for seasoning ... but the meal just melted away!

Steven How about calling for an air drop!

Me Carrier eagle?

Mom Can you write HELP in the snow?

Me I did that...and it's in yellow to show up better!

Marilyn Call Amazon, I'm sure they can drone something into you! This thread is hilarious!

Marilyn's comment actually set into motion the idea of capturing all these posts for a book chapter!

Timothy Jones
Monday, April 18 1:00 pm

Post: NOT GONNA HAPPEN TODAY. CAN'T GET ME OUT. Hopefully tomorrow. I'm eating paper and paste...just like in elementary school! Not bad, really.

[I posted photos of snow still coming down on property, taken from lodge deck]

Ray Too bad the barn cat is at the other camp. (Attached: link "9 Countries That Eat Cats and Dogs")

Sydna I find this completely disturbing, Mr. Ray. (Smile emoji) Glad June Bug is safe.

Me But you have to admit, this gives the term "cat lovers" a whole new meaning!

Ruth I hear fingers are good.

Me I'll start with toes. Less obvious when meeting new people and shaking hands. I don't have to wear sandals.

Ruth Now I'm actually consumed with the mental picture of you eating your appendages for a snack.

Ruth Are you hungry?

Ruth is getting back at me for teasing her about our long Colorado winters. She really LOVES them!

Bill Where's the cat?

Bill, seriously, where have you been for the last few days?

Me Fortunately—for June Bug—she's at the valley camp, probably enjoying a big bowl of her little kitty kibble. Man, that sounds good right now!

Timothy Jones
Monday, April 18 3:00 pm

Post: Found this candy bar ... have no idea how old it is. Don't even remember putting it in my supplies box. Starting with half of the Snickers Bar—the Snic part, as it happens, cutting it in two—trying to spread it out.

[I posted a photo of half a Snickers Bar]

Sydna (smiley face icon)

Les I'm sorry ... but having experience as a Marine, Snickers does not qualify as "roughing it."

Jim Tim, perhaps you need to look for the cat. I bet it tastes just like chicken.

Sydna Glad June Bug is safe from the likes of Mr. Jim!

Louise Candy! That's all you need. Even with a pantry and fridge full of food, I can tell you that from personal experience. Listen to your mother-in-law.

Had the second half for a late dinner. I'm now officially out of food ... no clean underwear either.

Monday, April 18 6:15 pm

POST BY MY WIFE, AND SOMETIMES TRAIL-HIKING BUDDY:
  Diane Dinner tonight. Wish Tim wasn't stuck in snow without food.
  [She posted a photo of the dinner table with a huge Thanksgiving-like spread, a cornucopia of food]
  Me My cute wife. Okay, that's cruel! Hilarious, but cruel.
  Linda Aw, you are so mean ... LOL!
  Amanda Oh, this is just sad! But I can't stop laughing!
  Gayle Diane, sure glad we live within walking distance from your home. Be right over.
  James Cold blooded. Love it!
  Julie I LOVE this Diane! You're devious (nothing wrong with that). Enjoy your sucker, Tim, if you have any left.
  Kevin You are an evil person.
  Me She's too much, isn't she?
  [I posted a hard-laughing emoji]
  James Good news! Paula Deen has pine tree bark recipes! You are saved!
  (link: Pine Bark: Paula Deen: Food Network)
  Me So nice of you think of me, James!
  [I posted a photo of a large plate of BBQ dinner, sent via Facebook Messenger by my son-in-law]
  Me You can't imagine how mean that is. Hope you choke on the brisket, not enough to kill you, but just enough to have someone stomp on your chest, repeatedly.
  Joe rofl (rolling on floor laughing)
  Me (another hard-laughing emoji)

Tuesday, April 19 7:30 am

WAS THAT BRIGHT SUNSHINE I SAW OUT MY CARETAKER quarter windows? Hadn't seen that in few days. Never so glad to hear the sound of the snowplow getting closer to camp. I was rescued!

It was nice of all my friends and family to be thinking of me while I was stranded on the top of a mountain. Supportive and entertaining, the exchanges made the isolation bearable. Grateful to all of them.

I finally got off the mountain around 2 pm, when my replacement arrived. That afternoon, I had just enough time to do some grocery shopping, wash my laundry and repack. I was due back up at the mountaintop camp the next morning. Forecast for the balance of the week: Snow and rain showers everyday through the next weekend, with a chance of thunder snow. Thunder snow? But, that's another story.

Chapter Thirty-Eight
STONES OF HEART

"Enjoy the little things in life ... for one day, you'll look back and realize they were the big things."—Anonymous

ON MANY TRAILS IN THE AMERICAN WEST

SEVERAL YEARS ago I started a tradition of collecting little rock mementos on my trail hikes and bringing them home to my wife. Okay, I know what some of you are thinking: If everyone did this, soon there would be no mountains left to climb, no trails to traverse. I think there's still enough out there. Some people collect seashells at the beach, and there are still beaches. I collect small rocks—but for a purpose.

For most of our married life, Diane and I have enjoyed hiking and trekking, especially when our kids were young. We've strolled miles of Southern California beaches, explored the tide pools, camped in the Yosemite Valley and in the desert, and adventured together across dozens of California, Colorado, Arizona, Washington and Utah trails. Diane hiked over 350 miles of the 486-mile Colorado Trail with me, until she blew out her knees ... probably because of the occasional 20-mile-plus sections. She encouraged me to continue, and I finished my last segment of this continuous trail from Denver to Durango, but, sadly, without her.

For the past few years, Diane has stayed home many times while I continue to hike the wilderness, especially the longer trips. She's done this partly for her knees' sake (and they thank her), but also because she provides in-home elder care to her mother (her father passed in March of 2015). She's supported and encouraged me to continue getting outdoors, knowing that hiking meets my need for grand adventure, quiet reflection and a spiritual, soul-healing connection with God's creation. I'm grateful.

Still, I have felt bad taking hikes without her, knowing how she would have loved being out there as well. I wanted her to know I was thinking about her and wished she could have come with me. So I decided I would bring back a piece of each hike to her, with perhaps a small related story as well. I would take home a small stone, and describe the location of the find, as well as other details of the hike.

These rock remembrances couldn't be just any stone. No random, organic-shaped rock would work, no matter how interesting. It had to be a thoughtful choice. It had to be the shape of a heart.

This turned out to be an ambitious commitment. How many heart-shaped stones do you think you see on a trail hike? Well, few, as it turns out. And you really have to search for them! I look for these heart shapes in dry creek beds, washes, eroded areas or streams, somewhere where the elements have tumbled, chipped, cracked and worn larger rocks down to smaller versions of their original selves.

These natural souvenirs cannot be too big (extra weight, limited backpack capacity) or too small (I've gotten home and can't even find *My Precious*, hidden away somewhere special in my clothes or pack for safety). And, of course, it has to look somewhat like a heart. My special-shaped choices have pushed the definition of heart at times, requiring a good bit of imagination, which, fortunately, Diane has, or at least she's been very kind.

For a while, Diane would write in marking pen the date and

location of the geological gift where she had been on my mind. After a point there were too many stones to keep up with. But each seemed special and appreciated by Diane, so eventually she gathered them up from dresser tops, side tables, kitchen counters and my hiking pants pockets, and put them all into a glass jar on a shelf in our bathroom. And now, she needs a bigger glass jar.

Perhaps one day when I can't get out any more, when I'm too old to collect trail rocks, we'll sit together on the couch and dump the touchstones of memories out of the jar. We'll retell the stories of the years of hiking, but more than that, we'll reaffirm our love for the outdoors, and for each other, glad that we're still on this journey together.

I think we are going to need a bigger jar!

Chapter Thirty-Nine
972,000 STEPS

"You are never too old to set another goal or dream a new dream."—C. S. Lewis

THE COLORADO TRAIL, DENVER TO DURANGO

I OPENED my packet with pride and anticipation. My suitable-for-framing certificate from the Colorado Trail Foundation had arrived. There was my name, and emblazoned across the top was the headline: "I completed the Colorado Trail." What a commitment of time. What a lot of work. What a dream come true.

This was a story years in the making, covering 486 mountainous miles, much of it above 10,000 feet. The trail is divided into 28 segments, and the challenge took Kevin, Diane, and me from Colorado's capitol city Denver to Durango in the southwest part of the state, passing through eight mountain ranges, six National Forests, six designated wilderness areas, along five river systems, and through some of Colorado's most beautiful country. And (as the certificate reads) the trail took us up a combined total of 89,354 vertical feet!

We didn't tackle this arduous trail as a "thru-hike," but broke it up into the recommended sections, getting out into the wilderness when we could. Diane did have to bail after a point, but Kevin and I continued all the way to our final segment, a fabulous 20.6 mile section with a 4,186 ft. elevation gain through the remote San Juan Wilderness in the southwest part of the state —one of my favorite hiking regions in all of Colorado.

As was often our pattern, for this last section, Kevin and I each parked our vehicles at the opposite trailheads of the segment and hiked toward each other. We met on the trail, shared notes and snacks, and continued on. When we arrive at our respective destinations, we have a vehicle waiting for us. We brought long-range walkie-talkies to connect at points along the way, but my radio decided to act up. Because we were at such a high elevation, we were able to text each other about our respective progress.

Kevin has a longer stride, and I stop too often for calendar-quality photos, so he usually beats me to the halfway point. About the time we did meet on the trail, it started to rain. Hard and long. We lost an hour huddled under large pines for cover, and eventually just had to start out again wrapped in our rain ponchos. My plastic covering goes down below my knees. I would have looked ridiculous marching down the trail, if there was anyone else there to see me. I know I appeared as a small green tent with legs and hiking boots sticking out the bottom. I have a selfie from this scene that both humors and disturbs me.

It took me 13 hours to complete this section, feet dragging to the SUV by sunset. No bragging rights for speed, but maybe some for endurance, especially since the last six miles were mostly uphill through alpine tundra above tree line. We had finished the whole Colorado Trail! And I now have the certificate to prove it.

In the days and weeks that followed, I'll have to admit that although I had a tremendous feeling of accomplishment and satisfaction, I also felt a bit of a let down. I had taken on this huge personal contest (with the help and support of Kevin and Diane) and with one of 972,000 hiking steps at a time, and had beaten this challenging trail. But now it was over. Both Kevin and I had similar emotions when we completed summiting all of the fourteeners in Colorado.

Am I done with adventuring? No way! I may not know exactly what that future looks like, but, like Forrest Gump, I just want to keep on running, er, hiking. As I get older, I may have to move more slowly on the trails, take more breaks, try harder not to fall down, be less risky and set realistic goals for my age. I guess that's true, regardless of any of our interests and activities —that is if we'd like to stay around a little longer. I'll keep doing what I love to do, as long as I can do it. And if I can't explore and experience the great outdoors as I once did, or in the way I'd like to continue, then I'll find another way. There are no hard and fast rules about how to enjoy the wilderness.

I suppose that with any of us, when we are able to finish a goal, there is that feeling of elation, but if you loved the journey, a tinge of disappointment as well. We finish to cheers and pats on the back—even if just our own satisfaction of a job well done —and the arduous task is completed. But what's next?

And what if we don't cross the goal line? Maybe health or sheer will failed, financial resources dried up, residence or family circumstances changed, jobs transitioned, or life just had other plans than the ones we made, despite our original intentions and efforts. The original dream wasn't realized. Then it's time to dream a new dream. There are no hard and fast rules for dreaming. Just takes a little imagination. And sometimes a measure of guts.

So, I'm looking for the next adventure, grand or small. The next dream. Join me in your own way. At my book signings, I write, "Try to go higher and farther!" This doesn't just apply to hiking and climbing. There may not be a certificate waiting at the end, but, oh, the reward. Even if it's just associated with the journey, one step at a time. And you'll have your own stories to tell.

ACKNOWLEDGMENTS

My sincerest thanks to all of those who came along side me on these wilderness explorations. Some of these were trail adventures; some were life adventures. Together, we've made memories for a lifetime.

Special thanks to my wife and friend Diane, who gave time and resources to support my writing, as well as my passion for the outdoors. I could not have done this without her backing, sacrifice and great content suggestions.

Many of the mostly-true tales told here originally appeared on my trail hiking blog site—expanded now for the book. Others are new accounts from the wild. A shout out to Ray Seldomridge for reading and editing my work. He makes me look better than I should.

My appreciation to Kevin J. Anderson and Rebecca Moesta of WordFire Press for this publishing opportunity as a follow-up to my first book, *Tales from the Trails*. Brother-in-law Kevin is also my hiking buddy that helps keeps an encouraging pace on the trails to try to get us to the car before dark.

ABOUT THE AUTHOR

T. Duren Jones (Tim), a former Periodicals Editorial and Art Director, has worked in marketing, advertising and publishing for more than 25 years. He currently works for the Broadmoor Hotel in Colorado Springs as a Wilderness Driver to the hotel's mountain camp properties (along with caretaking those camps in the winter off-season). Tim and Diane have raised four creative and equally adventurous children, and now are introducing the grandchildren to wondrous outdoor explorations in their home state of Colorado. Tim's first book, *Tales from the Trails*, is available on Amazon Books and from WordFire Press.

www.ingramcontent.com/pod-product-compliance
Lightning Source LLC
Chambersburg PA
CBHW031149020426
42333CB00013B/586